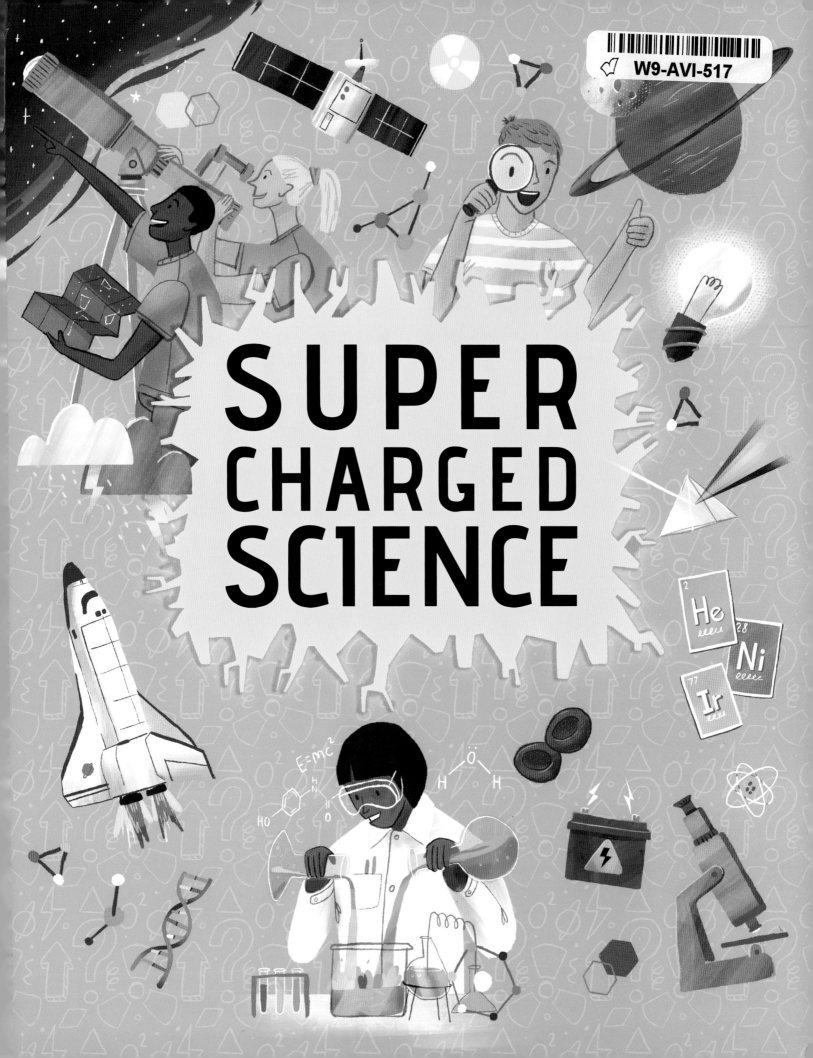

SUPER CHARGED SCIENCE

STEM+
SCIENCE TECHNOLOGY ENGINEERING MATHEMATICS

SUPER
CHARGED
SCIENCE

Written by
Lisa Regan

Illustrated by
Rhys Jefferys

ARCTURUS

ARCTURUS

This edition published in 2019 by Arcturus Publishing Limited
26/27 Bickels Yard, 151–153 Bermondsey Street,
London SE1 3HA, UK

Illustrated by Rhys Jefferys
Written by Lisa Regan
Edited by Becca Clunes and Donna Gregory
Designed by Supriya Sahai

ISBN: 978-1-78888-128-9
CH006209NT
Supplier 26, Date 1118, Print run 6847

Printed in China

What is STEM?
STEM is a world-wide initiative that aims to cultivate an
interest in Science, Technology, Engineering, and Mathematics,
in an effort to promote these disciplines to as wide a variety
of students as possible.

CONTENTS

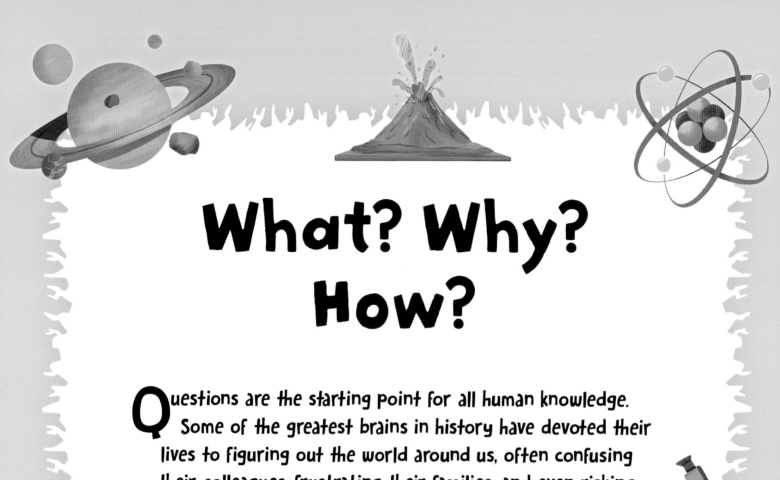

What? Why? How?

Questions are the starting point for all human knowledge. Some of the greatest brains in history have devoted their lives to figuring out the world around us, often confusing their colleagues, frustrating their families, and even risking imprisonment or death in the process.

An inquisitive mind is the most important tool in making new discoveries. If you're the sort of person that wonders what happens when someone switches on a light, or strikes a match, or uses a search engine, then science is the subject for you. However, to be a true scientist, you also need to be organized and methodical, and keep a record of your thoughts and findings to pass on to others. Do you have what it takes to join the trailblazers you will read about in this book?

OUR PLACE IN SPACE

The Moon orbits the Earth and the Earth orbits the Sun, along with seven other planets. They are all part of the Milky Way galaxy, which is just one of billions of galaxies in the Universe. We didn't always know that this was the case. Centuries of discoveries have allowed scientists to piece together this knowledge, using amazing inventions to look into space.

Scientists also know much more now about things closer to home. They understand how the Earth's rotation and gravity affect the atmosphere, winds, and ocean currents, and actions taking place deep inside the planet. It's literally a world of knowledge!

Looking Up

All humans throughout history have looked up to the sky and wondered what exactly is beyond our planet. Our knowledge of the cosmos has radically changed as our ability to see it has improved.

ANCIENT ASTRONOMERS

The Babylonians and Egyptians described the night skies in star charts more than 3,000 years ago. The Ancient Greeks developed these charts and named constellations—groups of stars that formed shapes in the sky. Claudius Ptolemy (100–170 CE) listed 48 constellations which we still recognize today. He also studied the visible planets, calling them "wandering stars," as they move in relation to the Sun and Earth at different times of the year.

Ptolemy thought that the Sun and planets revolved around the Earth. This belief continued until the middle of the 1500s.

A NEW VIEW

Nicolaus Copernicus (1473–1543) argued that the planets orbited the Sun. His observations were all made without a telescope. It was more than half a century later that Galileo Galilei (1564–1642) used a telescope to study other planets and the surface of our Moon. He looked more closely at Saturn and concluded that its "ears" were moons. Finally, in 1659, the Dutch astronomer Christiaan Huygens (1629–1695) saw that the "ears" were actually rings around the planet.

SEEING STARS

As telescopes improved, astronomers made more discoveries. William Herschel (1738-1822) was a musician and amateur astronomer who, working with his sister Caroline, built his own powerful telescope and studied comets and stars. In 1781, he discovered a planet beyond Saturn, which he named the Georgian star after the British King George III. We now know it as Uranus, named from Greek and Roman mythology like the other planets.

Saturn is one of the eight planets that orbit our Sun. In Galileo's time, people knew about only six of those planets.

Feeling hot, hot, HOT!

The Sun is a ball of gas made up of different layers, from a bright corona around the outer edge right through to a dense, hot core. Most of it is hydrogen, the lightest gas of all. In the core, the pressure is so great that the gas is squashed and fuses (joins) together to create the slightly heavier gas helium. This process is called nuclear fusion, and it causes the Sun to release energy. This energy is released as heat and light, which takes around eight minutes to reach Earth.

The Sun is actually a star! An expanding star is known as a red giant. A cooling, shrinking star is called a white dwarf.

STRUCK BY LIGHTNING

Did you know that lightning is five times hotter than the surface of the Sun? Lightning heats the air to an unbelievable temperature of 30,000°C (over 50,000°F), compared to the Sun's surface temperature of just 6,000°C (10,000°F). The Sun is still very, very hot though!

Uh-oh! Time's up!

OUT OF TIME

In about five billion years, the Sun will run out of hydrogen and fusion will stop. Its core will contract and the outer layers will cool and grow, giving off less light and heat. The Sun will eventually shrink and become cold and dark.

The Sun's outer atmosphere is called the corona. It can be seen during a total eclipse.

HOTSPOTS

There are cool and hot areas on the surface of the Sun. The cool areas appear darker and are called sunspots. Sometimes, energy builds up around these sunspots and is released as a bright flash, or solar flare. These solar flares send particles far into space. We are protected by our planet's atmosphere, but the particles can affect radio communications here on Earth.

In a Spin

The Earth moves around the Sun, but it also turns on its own axis, like a basketball spinning on a finger. This movement makes the Sun appear to rise in the East and set in the West every day, giving us day and night.

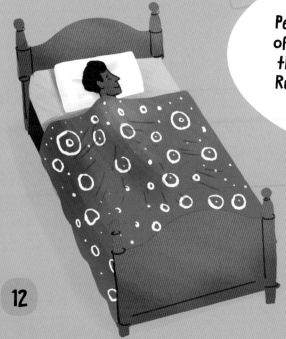

FASTER, FASTER!

The Earth is spinning much faster at the equator (about 1,650 km/h or 1,000 mph) than at the poles. Imagine looking down on the top of the Earth from space. A person standing near the North Pole for a day would hardly move at all, while a person standing on the equator would travel a vast distance in 24 hours.

People who live on opposite sides of the world never see the sun at the same time—when it's light in Russia, it's the middle of night in the United States!

PENDULUM PROOF

The Earth takes 24 hours to spin on its own axis. Early experiments involved dropping weights from tall buildings to prove that the Earth rotated. The weights did not land directly beneath, but slightly to one side, because of the movement of the planet. Léon Foucault (1819–1868) famously showed this in 1851 with one of science's most simple experiments—a pendulum that did not simply swing from side to side, but in a star shape.

Foucault showed off his pendulum experiment in a grand way. He suspended it on a 67-m-long wire hanging from the domed roof of the Panthéon in Paris.

Foucault also carried out important experiments to calculate the speed of light, and he invented the gyroscope. As a teenager, his teachers said he was lazy!

INTO SPACE

There are eight planets moving around the Sun. Earth is the third one, and it takes just over 365 days (one Earth year) to complete a full journey. Mercury and Venus are closer to the Sun, so their year is shorter. The planets that are farther away have longer distances to travel. A Mars year is over 680 days long. Neptune, the farthest planet, takes over 248 Earth years to travel around the Sun!

The sky's the limit!

The Earth is surrounded by the atmosphere—layers of gases that allow us to breathe, protect us from the Sun, and keep the Earth warm enough for living things to survive. Sometimes, streams of air rush around in the atmosphere, causing the turbulence that can make a plane drop dramatically as it flies.

JET STREAMS

The air gets colder as you climb higher, which is why mountains can have snow on top even in hot countries.

The closest layer to Earth is called the troposphere. It extends from Earth's surface to about 10 km up in the sky (around 6.2 miles, or 33,000 feet). Planes climb higher than this layer to avoid clouds and storms, but often encounter turbulence as they pass through jet streams on the border between the troposphere and the stratosphere.

RAIN OR SHINE

Most types of clouds form in the troposphere, so that is where the weather happens. Winds swirl from place to place, and rain and snow fall from the clouds. Before the eighteenth century, scientists could only study the atmosphere by climbing a mountain to get as high as possible. The invention of the hot air balloon allowed scientists to observe and measure conditions high above the Earth.

The Montgolfier brothers invented the hot air balloon in France, and made their first flight in 1783.

HIGHER AND HIGHER

The layers of the atmosphere are divided by their temperature. The stratosphere is comparatively warm. It contains lots of ozone gas which helps to protect us from the Sun's rays by absorbing dangerous ultraviolet (UV) radiation. Above that is the mesosphere, where the temperature falls as low as -90°C (-130°F). This is the layer where specks of space dirt (meteors) burn up as shooting stars.

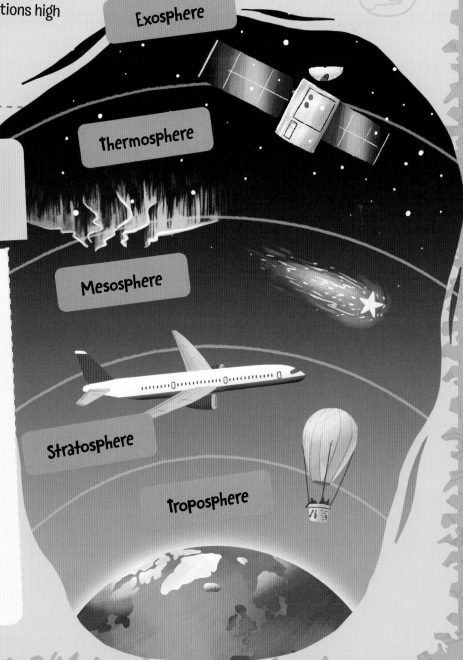

Exosphere

Thermosphere

Mesosphere

Stratosphere

Troposphere

A watery world

About 71% of Earth's surface is covered in water, and most of that water is ocean. Geographers divide it into five areas (the Pacific, Atlantic, Indian, Arctic, and Southern oceans) but in reality, they are all connected as one large, joined-up body of water. Marine animals can swim freely around them all. The ocean has fast-moving surface currents and deep-water currents, which move more slowly.

DUCKS ON TOUR

In 1992, a shipping container lost its cargo of 28,000 rubber ducks. They floated off in the Pacific ocean. The ducks have since been spotted halfway around the world, carried by ocean currents. Their locations help scientists to track how and where these currents flow.

The Southern Ocean is the "newest" named ocean. The idea of giving it a name was proposed in the year 2000.

SPINNING AROUND

The currents are caused by wind, temperature, and the spinning effect of the Earth. As the Earth turns on its axis, it makes the moving water veer off course. Instead of following a straight path, it gets shifted to the right (in the Northern hemisphere) or the left (in the Southern hemisphere). It is like a person wobbling sideways as they try to walk in a straight line across a spinning carousel.

The swirling effect of the Earth's rotation is called the Coriolis force, named after the nineteenth-century French mathematician who first explained it.

WORLD WEATHER

Ocean currents have a big effect on the weather. Some carry warm water into cold areas, warming up coastal countries. Other currents cause huge storms called tropical cyclones or hurricanes. Warm air over the ocean swirls at high speeds, twisted by the rotation of the planet. The storms grow stronger and move toward the land, causing giant waves, floods, and violent winds.

Light-years away

The Universe—it's an enormous idea, and hard to imagine. So what actually IS it? It is, literally, everything we can see, measure, or detect using technology—stars, galaxies, dust, light, and heat. It includes our solar system and far, far beyond.

MADE TO MEASURE

The universe is almost unthinkably vast. It would take a supersonic fighter plane more than a million years just to fly to the nearest star to the Sun. Earth's closest planet, Mars, is at least 56 million km (34 million miles) away. Scientists choose not to measure these distances in miles as there are too many zeroes involved. Instead, they use astronomical units (AU) and light-years. An AU is the distance between Earth and the Sun, or 150 million km (93 million miles).

A light-year is the distance the light travels in one year. It is about 9 trillion km, or nearly 6 trillion miles.

GROWING AND GROWING

The American astronomer Edwin Hubble (1889–1953) made an astonishing discovery in 1925. Using telescopes, he found that the universe contained many more galaxies than our own. Until then, it was thought that the Milky Way was the only one. A few years later he shocked the scientific world once again. He showed that the galaxies were moving away from each other. The universe is expanding, and all the stars and planets are getting farther apart.

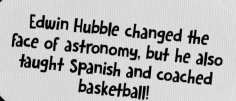

Edwin Hubble changed the face of astronomy, but he also taught Spanish and coached basketball!

WRITTEN IN THE STARS

Hubble's discoveries were so important that his name was given to a special space telescope, launched in 1990. This telescope has allowed us to observe the expanding universe. Imagine a blob of chocolate-chip cookie dough, where the chocolate chips are evenly spaced out. If you roll it out, the chips get farther apart—that's a bit like what's happening to our universe! Measuring the growth rate allows scientists to calculate how old the universe is. Most currently think that it is 13.8 billion years old.

Drifting by

The Earth and planets orbit the Sun, Moons orbit their planet, and artificial satellites orbit the Earth, beaming down videos and images that we see in our modern, everyday lives. But why don't all of these items just drift around in space?

The ISS (International Space Station) travels at a speed of around 27,600 km/h (17,150 mph) over 400 km (250 mi) above the Earth.

GRAVITY DOES IT

The reason everything isn't floating around aimlessly is simple—gravity. Large objects, like Earth, have this invisible force that pulls things toward them. It stops your phone from floating up in the air, and it drags it to the ground with a bump and a smash if you drop it. Small objects have gravity, too, but too weak for you to notice. An object the size of a planet has enough gravitational pull to keep things in orbit around it, such as a moon or a satellite.

INTO SPACE ...

If you throw a ball as far as you can, it keeps moving until the Earth's gravity pulls it down. The harder you throw it, the farther it travels before it falls. A rocket has to move fast enough to pull away from this gravity so it can make its journey into space. The first rockets were launched in the 1950s, and by 1957 the Soviet Union (now known as Russia) had put the very first artificial satellites into orbit.

A satellite in low orbit (not too far from Earth) circles the planet about 15 times a day.

SOLAR POWER

An orbiting body must travel at a speed that is fast enough to keep it in orbit, but not so fast that it breaks away and flies off into space. Artificial satellites are often powered by rechargeable batteries that collect energy from the Sun. The ISS has thousands of solar cells to convert light into electricity. They cover an area half the size of a football field and can move so they always face the Sun.

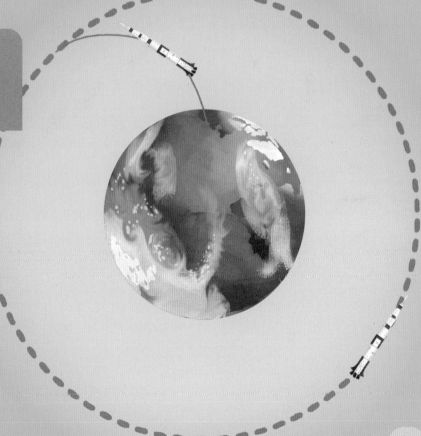

Over the Moon

On a clear night, you can see the Moon glowing in the sky above us. You might not know that it's gradually getting farther away! It is moving away from Earth at about 4cm (1.5 in) each year. That's about the same rate that your fingernails grow. So, how important is the Moon to us here on Earth?

RISING TIDES

The Moon is kept in place by the Earth's gravitational pull, but it has its own gravity too. This pulls more strongly on the closest side of the planet, and less on the farthest side. It creates a bulge in the oceans, because they are most-easily moved part of the Earth. Since the Earth is rotating at the same time, this gravitational pull causes high tides twice every day, with low tides in between.

The bulging tides are a little like pressing a soft beach ball and seeing the air inside squash out to the edges.

THE DARK SIDE

No human had seen the far side of the Moon before 1959, when the Russian spacecraft Luna 3 sent back photographs. It does not have the dark spots that form the face of "the man in the moon," but it does have lots of craters. It is called the "dark side" of the Moon because we cannot see it, but it still receives light from the Sun, so it's not really dark at all.

Saturn is famous for its rings, but it was also the second distant planet discovered to have moons around it. Five were named between 1655 and 1686.

MANY MOONS AGO

Our planet is not the only one with a moon orbiting around it. Mars has two of its own, and the giant outer planets have lots. More are being discovered all the time, but the first were identified way back in 1610 by Galileo. He saw four of Jupiter's many moons. One of them, Ganymede, is the largest moon in the solar system. It is bigger than the planet Mercury!

MYTH BUSTERS

Science is built on proposing theories and testing to see if they are right or wrong, before suggesting new theories to take their place. Sometimes, people have definitely been barking up the wrong tree ...

The Sun isn't yellow!

As children, we draw the Sun as a large yellow circle. That's how it looks to us here on Earth. And yet, seen from space, the Sun is really white. Its light splits into different wavelengths, from red to blue, which we can see in a rainbow. Our planet's atmosphere scatters some of these wavelengths, leaving only the yellow, when the Sun is high in the sky. At sunrise and sunset, when the Sun is near the horizon, we see more orange and red.

STRANGE BUT TRUE!
Scientists believe that giant planets such as Neptune and Uranus have their own stash of micro-diamonds, which fall as rain.

Diamonds aren't made of coal!

Crystal-clear diamonds and jet black coal are both made of carbon. So, can coal be super squashed and turned into diamonds? No! Most diamonds are far older than the plants that coal was formed from. They were made deep in the Earth's mantle, at high temperatures and under great pressure. Geologists believe that they are forced to the surface by volcanic eruptions. Coal, on the other hand, was formed when dead plants were compressed in prehistoric swamps.

WHERE LIFE BEGAN

Scientists working in various fields, from biology and geology to engineering, have helped to paint a picture of life long ago. Secrets hidden in the layers of rock beneath our feet reveal clues about extinct species, ancient landscapes, and how the climate and atmosphere have changed over millions of years of Earth's history.

They are not the only things to have changed. The animals and plants living today are different from those that existed long ago. Their remains show us how living things evolved from early beginnings to what we see today.

If reading this gives you goosebumps, it's a throwback to when early humans had longer body hair, like our cousins the chimpanzees. Animals with lots of fur can make themselves look bigger when it stands on end. You hardly have any hair, but your follicles still stand to attention!

Relics of the past

Fossils tell us about plants and animals that lived long ago. Fossils can be actual parts of living things such as leaves or bones and teeth, or items made and left by animals, such as footprints, bite marks, nests, and even animal dung (called coprolites).

HOW THEY LIVED

Dinosaur tracks make good fossils. They can tell us the size of a dinosaur and its stride length, whether the creatures walked on two legs or four, whether they lived in herds, and how fast they moved. Other lifestyle fossils (called trace fossils) give more clues about a creature's habits, diet, and actions. Body fossils are usually made from hard parts such as bones, claws, teeth, and shells. If a dinosaur scientist (a paleontologist) is really lucky, he or she might find fossils of softer parts such as skin, muscles, or feathers.

Fossils of dinosaur eggs have been found in more than 200 places. The first were found in France in 1859.

FOSSIL FORMATION

Only a fraction of living creatures have been preserved as fossils. Most die and then are eaten or rot away. If, however, a plant or animal is buried by mud or sand, it may form a fossil. Water seeps into the body parts (for example, a leg bone) and replaces the bone with other chemicals. Millions of years later, the layers of rock are worn away by wind and rain to reveal a bone-shaped object for us to find and study.

AWAY AT SEA

The best conditions for making fossils are usually under the ocean. Layer upon layer of sand piles on top of dead creatures and preserves them. Eventually, the rocks are pushed to the surface (in earthquakes or when mountains are formed) and the fossils are exposed. Some land creatures were washed into the water when they died and were preserved in the same way, but a huge proportion of fossils are of sea creatures such as ammonites and trilobites.

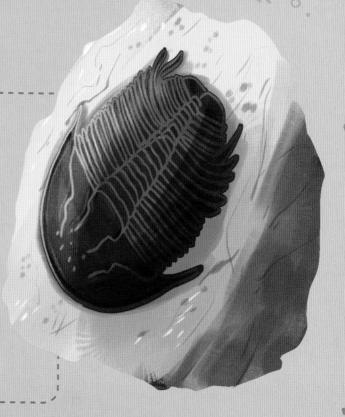

Dragons or dinosaurs?

No one knew dinosaurs existed until specific bones were identified in the 1800s. Before then, many people thought that the bones belonged to such creatures as dragons, griffins, and even giants from mythology and folklore.

EARLY FINDS

Most early bone discoveries were made by people collecting them as a hobby. The sciences of geology and paleontology were still relatively new when, in the 1820s, Megalosaurus and Iguanodon were found and named. The first nearly complete skeleton was uncovered in 1838 by William Parker Foulke in New Jersey, USA. Sir Richard Owen (1804–1892) noticed that the fossils had common characteristics, and proposed a new group of large, extinct, land-based reptiles which he named dinosaurs (in 1842).

Flying reptiles, such as pterosaurs, and swimming ones, such as plesiosaurs and ichthyosaurs, were not dinosaurs, as they did not live on land.

LIFE ON EARTH

Owen's dinosaurs were land-dwelling reptiles with stiff, upright legs and five vertebrae (spine bones) joined together near the hips. It is now known that they lived between 230 and 65 million years ago, in a time known as the Mesozoic Era. They shared the planet with many other creatures—insects such as dragonflies and bees, reptiles such as crocodiles and lizards, and sharks and other fish. Early mammals such as cynodonts had also evolved from reptiles, about 260 million years ago.

TAKING OFF

The first known bird was Archaeopteryx, discovered in the early 1860s. It formed a link between dinosaurs and modern birds.

Startling discoveries show us that although dinosaurs became extinct, they left some very familiar descendants in the form of birds. Fossil finds in China in the 1990s revealed that plenty of dinosaurs had feathers. Small, two-legged theropods such as Velociraptor had the correct hip-shape to evolve into modern birds. Their face bones fused to become a beak, and their body size shrank to allow them to fly.

What are we made of?

You may find the answer surprising. Humans are mostly made of water! In fact, so are most living things. People are nearly 60% water, apples are 84% water, and jellyfish are 95% water!

DOUBLE TROUBLE

Living things are called organisms and are made of cells. These cells contain DNA, a protein that carries the genetic code—a set of instructions that controls what organisms look like and how they behave. Much of our DNA is shared with other creatures. Less than 0.1% makes you different from the person next to you (the shade of your hair and eyes, for example). You are even 96% genetically similar to a chimp, and 90% similar to a cat.

A full set of genetic instructions for one living thing is known as the genome.

ALL LIFE IS CONNECTED

Since the human genome was first mapped out in 2003, scientists have compared it to the genome of lots of other organisms. There are some similarities in all living things, and it is because we all evolved from the same ancestor—a single-celled organism that existed more than 3 billion years ago and gave rise to all of life on Earth. The relationship between organisms can be shown on a kind of evolutionary family tree, known as the Tree of Life.

LET'S GET THIS SORTED

Biologists study living things. They separate them into kingdoms (such as plants, animals, and fungi). Each kingdom is divided into smaller and smaller groups, keeping the most similar organisms together in families and species. The modern system of grouping and naming species was developed by the Swedish naturalist Carl Linnaeus (1707–1778). He was a keen collector of plant and animal specimens, and thought it was vital to have an agreed-upon, standard way for all scientists to refer to them.

Giants!

We share our beautiful planet with millions of amazing creatures, from tiny insects to massive mammals. How do some animals grow to such enormous sizes? It is an intriguing question for biologists and paleontologists studying both prehistoric and modern-day beasts.

Prehistoric dragonfly relatives had wings measuring around 70 cm (more than 2 ft) across. As oxygen levels decreased, they evolved to become smaller.

MEGA MONSTERS

Long before the dinosaurs, the Earth was home to a range of huge insects such as dragonflies and cockroaches. Like the bugs of today, they had no lungs; instead, insects collect oxygen through holes in their body (called spiracles) and pass it to their cells. Around 300 million years ago, the atmosphere contained over 30% oxygen (much higher than today's levels of 21%). The spiracles could take in enough oxygen to supply even a supersized insect's needs.

GREEN GIANTS

One of today's most amazing plants evolved from prehistoric grasses between 30 and 40 million years ago—bamboo. It is the world's fastest growing plant; some types grow up to 90 cm (35 in) in a single day. The giants of the tree world are sequoias, one of the oldest living things on Earth. Their ancestors were widely found during dinosaur times, but they have evolved to live in a tiny part of California, where the oldest are 3,500 years old and up to 95 m (300 ft) high.

WHAT A WHOPPER

The Mesozoic era had its own giants, such as Diplodocus and Brachiosaurus, which grew up to 27 m (90 ft) and around 40 tons. These are dwarfed by the blue whale—the largest animal ever. It can be 30 m (100 ft) long and weigh 180 tons. Biologists think it evolved to be so large during an ice age around 2.6 million years ago. The oceans at this time were filled with an excess of krill, feeding the whales and allowing them to get bigger and bigger.

A closer look

Around 96% of animals have eyes, and they take many different forms. All of them are thought to have developed from one "proto-eye" that evolved as many as 540 million years ago. Today's animals have an astonishing range of vision.

ONE VISION?

Early eyes simply detected light and darkness, but small, gradual improvements in different special areas gave creatures new advantages in the evolutionary race. Some eyes are good at judging distance, while others can see 360 degrees around them. Lots of creatures can see ultraviolet and infrared light that humans cannot detect. As eyesight evolved, so did another thing—camouflage. Animals needed to use their patterns to stay hidden.

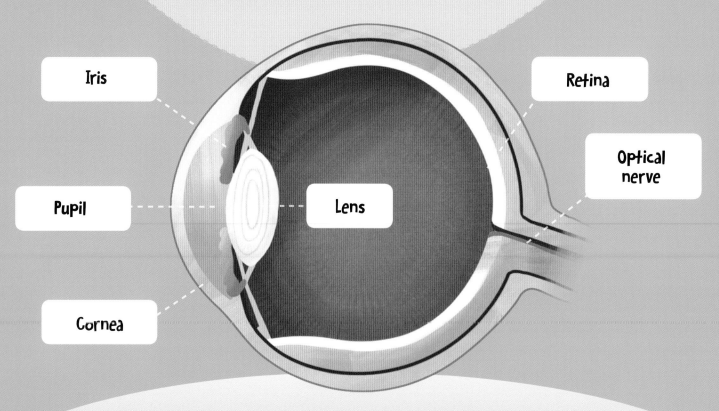

Iris

Retina

Optical nerve

Pupil

Lens

Cornea

This is a human eye. Light enters the cornea, goes through the iris, then the pupil, and then it bends through the lens to focus, upside down, on the retina. The image is "sent" down the optical nerve to the brain, where the image is flipped!

DO YOU SEE WHAT I SEE?

There are two types of light receptors on the retina. The first kind are called "rods" and they work best in very dim light. Humans have far fewer rods than cats and horses, so our night vision is poor compared to theirs. These animals, though, do not see a world of brilliant daytime hues like we do. They have fewer of the second kind of receptors, called cones, so they can see shades of blue and green much better than reds and pinks.

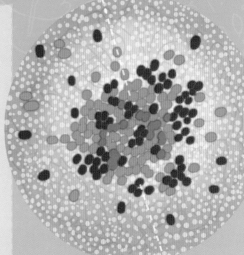

Cones

Rods

BUG EYES

Most insects have five eyes, but some have just two compound eyes with thousands of lenses (4,000 for a housefly and around 30,000 for a dragonfly). It is like having lots of tiny eyes looking in different directions. Evolution has provided lots of ways for creatures to see all around. A chameleon can move both eyes in opposite directions. Snails' and lobsters' eyes are on stalks to wiggle wherever they like. Prey animals such as deer and horses have their eyes at the sides, so they can see behind them.

A tarsier's eye is as big as its brain! At the same body-to-eye ratio, your eye would be the size of a grapefruit.

Pass it on

Genes give your body instructions for growing, developing, and staying alive. They control every tiny thing about your body—how tall you'll be, the shape of your nose, the size of your feet! Genes determine how much melanin is in the hair, eyes, and skin, changing how dark or pale those features are. We inherit half of them from our mother and the other half from our father.

GENETIC REVOLUTION

Lots of creatures' genes have evolved over time to help them survive in the wild. The peppered moth is an amazing example of this! During the Industrial Revolution, when the air became dark and heavy with smog, the number of black peppered moths increased. Some scientists think that the moths' genes adapted to the new, darker environment, making the moths darker so that birds would find them harder to spot.

CHANGING TIMES

Changes, or mutations, in genes affect future generations. Harmful mutations often die out and are left behind. Helpful mutations pass from parent to child, making the next generations stronger and more likely to survive. This process is known as natural selection, and it drives evolution. The idea was first proposed by Charles Darwin (1809–1882), and it was revolutionary. Today, we know how it applies to plants, insects, birds, and even humans—but he was widely criticized for his ideas.

HEY, BLUE EYES

Sometime between 6,000 and 10,000 years ago, a genetic blip partially switched off the coding that makes eyes brown. It is thought that all blue-eyed people have this first blue-eyed ancestor in common. What is not clear is why the mutation spread. Evolution chooses mutations that help the organism to live in a particular environment to continue through generations. It may be that blue eyes, and the lighter skin that usually accompanies them, were helpful for survival in cold countries. Scientists are still trying to figure it out.

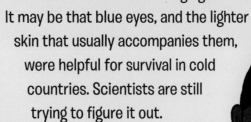

Getting around

All animals and plants that we know today evolved from single-celled organisms that lived in the water. Around 1.5 billion years ago, these cells changed, and many became the ancestors of animals—who now know lots of different ways to move and groove around the Earth!

MAKING MOVES

Plants, animals, and fungi followed their own evolutionary paths. Only animals found ways of moving around—on land, in the air and in the ocean. It is thought that the first four-legged creatures lived in shallow water around 397 million years ago, before making a move onto land. Scientists studying fossils can see what features developed or were lost on the way to the animals that live on Earth today.

Some creatures have leftover features (called vestigial features) that give clues about how they evolved.

LEGLESS LIZARDS

Snakes evolved from lizard-like creatures and had both front and back legs around 150 million years ago. Over the course of time, they lost these legs to make it easier for them to burrow underground. Scientists have found that some snakes have tiny bones where their back legs once were. Some pythons even have small back claws sticking out of their skin. Genetic tests show that the gene still exists for snakes to grow legs.

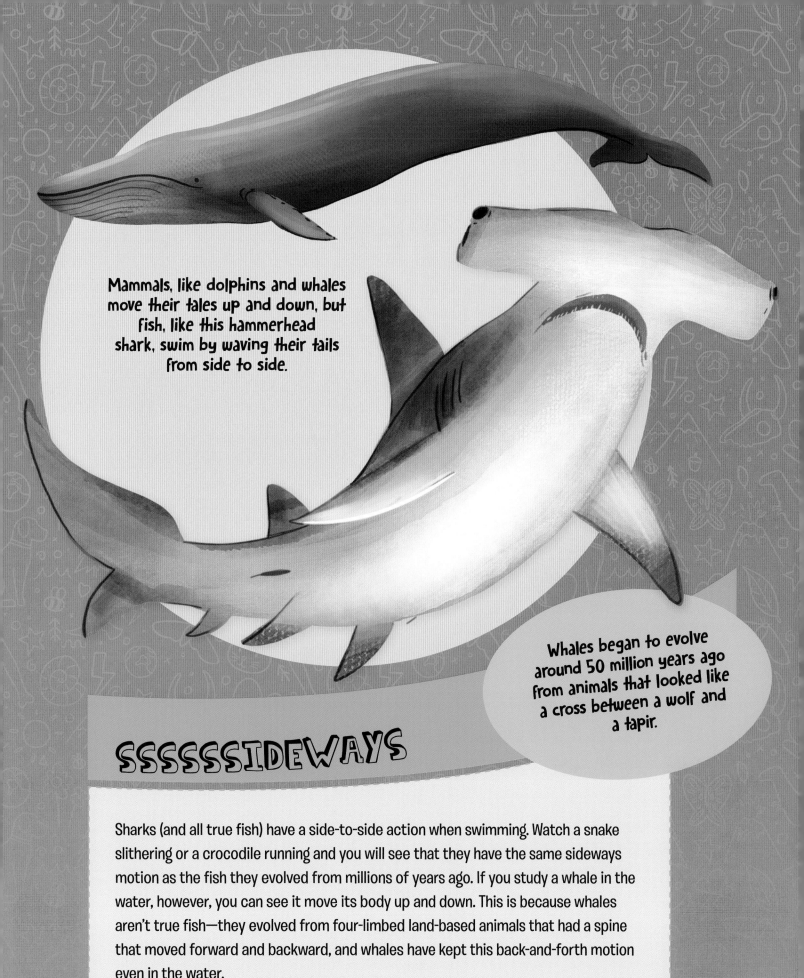

Mammals, like dolphins and whales move their tales up and down, but fish, like this hammerhead shark, swim by waving their tails from side to side.

Whales began to evolve around 50 million years ago from animals that looked like a cross between a wolf and a tapir.

SSSSSSIDEWAYS

Sharks (and all true fish) have a side-to-side action when swimming. Watch a snake slithering or a crocodile running and you will see that they have the same sideways motion as the fish they evolved from millions of years ago. If you study a whale in the water, however, you can see it move its body up and down. This is because whales aren't true fish—they evolved from four-limbed land-based animals that had a spine that moved forward and backward, and whales have kept this back-and-forth motion even in the water.

World domination

If the Mesozoic Era was the age of the dinosaurs, then the Cenozoic Era in which we now live is often described as the age of mammals. However, in reality, our six-legged insect friends make up most of our world!

NUMBER CRUNCHING

If success is judged by sheer numbers, then invertebrates win the race. As many as 97% of all animals are invertebrates (animals without a backbone). Insects form the largest part of this group, with an estimated 1 million different species. That's around 80% of all the world's animal species alive today, compared to a mere 5,500 species of mammal.

HAPPY TOGETHER

There are fewer species of ant than of beetles, but ants appear in far greater numbers. They live in gatherings called colonies that can contain thousands or even millions of ants working together. Scientists estimate that as many as a million trillion ants live on this planet. Like all other insects, they are essential to the ecosystem. They dispose of waste such as dead fruit and animals, they carry seeds and dig dirt, and they eat pests.

There are more species of beetle than any other insect. Scientists have named around 400,000 different species.

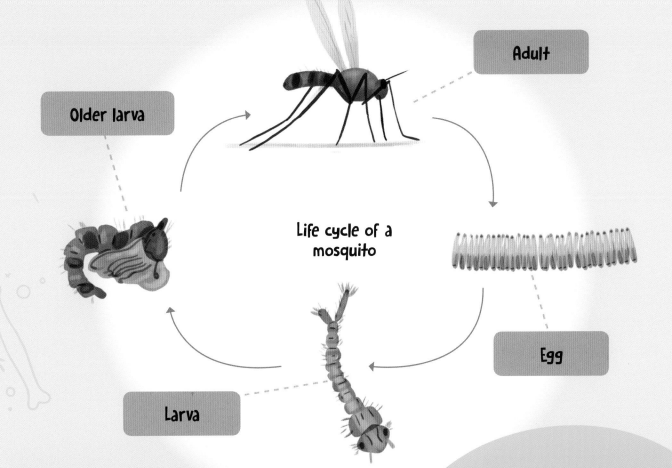

Older larva

Adult

Life cycle of a
mosquito

Egg

Larva

LIFE CYCLES

An insect lives a fascinating life, although it is
sometimes very short. Starting as an egg, it hatches into
a wiggly, bug-like larva that looks nothing like its adult
version. The main insect groups then go through a pupa
stage inside a protective casing before coming out as an
adult. Some insects, such as dragonflies, skip the pupa
stage. Their larvae (called nymphs) look more like mini-
adults. The larval stage can last for four years, and their
adult life might be only a few months.

Studies suggest that
there are more than 200 million
insects for every person on
Earth! No wonder scientists are
studying how to farm them for
humans to eat.

MYTH BUSTERS

There are still things that science can't confirm about ancient animals and human ancestors, but here are two myths that they're certain about.

Sauropods <u>didn't</u> live in the water!

Some prehistoric creatures, like plesiosaurs, ichthyosaurs, and mosasaurs, spent their whole lives in the water. They were reptiles, but they were not dinosaurs. At one time, scientists suggested that some dinosaurs were also water creatures. Sauropods—huge, long-necked plant-eaters, such as Brachiosaurus—were often shown in illustrations swimming in lakes. Evidence has proved this wrong for various reasons. Their footprints have only been found on land, their lungs were not designed for life in the water, and their bodies, although huge, were light enough that they would have floated!

Humans <u>didn't</u> evolve from chimpanzees!

Humans and apes, such as gorillas and chimps evolved from a common ancestor that lived millions of years ago. That ancestor is now extinct, along with other human relatives (called hominids). Somewhere between 5 and 8 million years ago, we evolved into separate species. So, chimpanzees are our (very) distant cousins, but definitely not our great-great-great ... grandparents!

USE THE FORCE!

You cannot see forces, but you can see their effects all around you. Forces make things move, they squash and stretch things, and they even make things float, fly, and fall.

Forces can be applied directly when objects come into contact with each other. Giving your brother a push on the swing or falling to the ground both involve forces (sometimes, science hurts!). Forces can also take effect at a distance. Magnetic forces don't require objects to touch, and gravity can pull objects that are vast distances from each other, such as the Sun and planets.

Forces are "fun"damental to physics. They put the fun into everything, from football to skydiving to simply lying down in your bed.

Airheads

It may seem silly to talk about weighing air, but scientists spent many years trying to work out how to do just that. Air is constantly pushing on us and the things around us ... but we just don't feel it!

PUMP IT UP

In the Middle Ages, engineers could build pumps to move water upward by 10m (33 feet), but no higher. No one had any idea why! Then, in the 1640s, an Italian scientist called Evangelista Torricelli had a bright idea. He wrote to a friend, saying, "We live submerged at the bottom of an ocean of the element air." Everything on Earth is squashed down by the weight of that "ocean." So, how does a pump work?

A pump works by taking away the weight of air that is pushing the water down.

44

UNDER PRESSURE

French scientist Blaise Pascal continued Torricelli's investigation. In 1648, he asked his brother-in-law Florin to conduct an experiment with two tubes of mercury. Florin left one tube near his home—and nothing happened to it. He carried the other tube up a mountain. The higher he went, the more the mercury rose up the tube. Why? Because there was less air above the tube to push down on it!

The mercury tube worked as a pressure-measuring device—and it became known as a barometer. Today, barometers are still used to predict the weather.

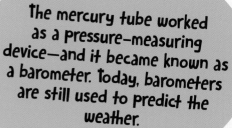

AIR POWER

In 1650, a German inventor called Otto von Guericke showed just how strong air pressure is by building a new kind of air pump. He fitted two iron hemispheres (half spheres) together and sucked the air out. After that, no one could get them apart ... not even two teams of strong horses! The hemispheres were pushed closed by the air pressure around them. There was nothing inside pushing the other way, so they stayed shut tight!

Forceful friction

Lots of different things affect the way the universe works. Physicists study forces, which push or pull on things around them. Friction is one of these forces, and it affects the way we move every day.

SMOOTHLY DOES IT

Friction is a force that acts against an object trying to move, making movement more difficult. Try pushing a book across your desk. It will slide fairly easily because the surfaces are smooth. Now try pushing the book along the carpet. It is harder to do, because one surface is rough, creating more friction.

ON THE MOVE

Friction can be used to stop things slipping and sliding. The soles of your shoes have bumps to give you "grip," or increase friction. When you apply the brakes on your bike, brake pads press against the moving wheel and cause enough friction to slow the wheel and then stop it completely. Somotimes, we want the opposite effect. Putting oil on a bicycle chain reduces friction so that it moves more smoothly, making it easier to pedal.

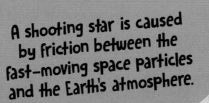

A shooting star is caused by friction between the fast-moving space particles and the Earth's atmosphere.

A wet match is harder to strike because water reduces friction between the two surfaces.

QUITE STRIKING

Rubbing your hands together causes friction between your palms. Holding them together uses no energy, but working against friction to make them move requires more energy from you. This energy is converted into heat, making your hands feel warm. The same thing happens when someone strikes a match. The rough edge of the matchbox increases friction and causes a spark, which lights the chemicals in the head of the match.

Pushing through

Moving through air and water creates friction, which slows things down. This is known as "drag," and it affects all moving objects, from baseballs to racing cars to swimmers.

AIR RESISTANCE

An object with a large surface area is slowed by more air pushing against it. Imagine dropping a flat piece of paper with one hand, and a scrunched-up piece with the other. The flat paper will fall more slowly because of its bigger surface area. Now fold the paper into a plane and drop it, nose down. It will plummet to the ground, as you have reduced the size of the surface cutting through the air. This is known as streamlining.

VROOM! VROOM!

NOT SO FAST

It is easy to see air resistance in action when you watch skydivers leap from a plane. The force of gravity pulls them toward the ground. When they open up their parachute, the canopy increases the air resistance to work against gravity and reduce the speed of the fall. In drag racing, the streamlined cars hurtle forward at great speed. When they cross the finish line, they eject parachutes at the rear to slow them much faster than applying brakes.

NATURE'S LEAD

Streamlined shapes are frequently seen in nature. A falcon diving through the air folds back its wings to reduce its own surface area. Penguins and sharks glide through the water with ease, thanks to their pointed shape and smooth surface. People have copied these shapes to make cars, planes, and submarines faster and more efficient. One of the greatest names to use these principles was not a scientist, but a designer called Raymond Loewy, nicknamed the "Father of streamlining."

Double parachutes safely slow drag racing cars from over 539 km/h (335 mph) to a stop.

The gravity of the situation

One force that acts on you all the time is gravity. It pulls on everything around you—your homework, your sandwich, your games console—clearly it is very important! Gravity stops your sandwich from floating away, and it keeps you seated to do your homework and play games.

VITAL FOR LIFE

Gravity is a force that pulls objects toward each other. All objects exert gravity, but only huge objects, such as planets and stars, have enough force to make much difference. The Earth's gravity acts on gas molecules in the atmosphere, keeping the atmosphere close to our surface. Smaller planets with less gravitational force cannot always keep hold of an atmosphere. The Sun is so enormous that its gravity is enough to hold in place all the planets of the solar system.

Saturn is a really big planet, and exerts enough gravity to hold no fewer than 53 moons!

THINKING AROUND THE PROBLEM

Isaac Newton (1642–1727) revolutionized the way scientists thought about gravity. In the early 1600s, astronomer Johannes Kepler (1571–1630) had described the motion of planets around the Sun, but Newton was perturbed about what kept them in place. Why did they travel in elliptical orbits (the oval paths that the planets follow) rather than straight lines? He figured that a pulling force must be acting upon them, and also on all the moons that orbit the planets.

UNIVERSAL THEORY

Newton set out his Theory of Universal Gravitation in 1666, explaining the relationship between gravitational force and distance. What made it so revolutionary was that he worked out that gravity is everywhere, between all objects, but it depends upon mass. His law explains that gravity increases as the mass of the object increases, but decreases as the distance gets bigger. It describes both the downward force acting on us on Earth, and the force acting between objects in space.

Weight a minute

Weight is a force caused by gravity. It would change if you were somewhere with more or less gravity than Earth. It is often confused with mass, which stays the same wherever you might travel.

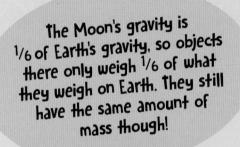

The Moon's gravity is 1/6 of Earth's gravity, so objects there only weigh 1/6 of what they weigh on Earth. They still have the same amount of mass though!

MASS-TER THE MEANINGS

We often mix up the terms weight and mass, but they are different things. Mass is how much "stuff" a thing is made of. It will only change if you add or remove some "stuff." Cutting a slice of cake reduces the mass of the cake, but eating too much cake adds to your mass in the long term! You could transport that cake to the Moon, and its mass would remain the same.

WEIGHT LOSS

Things weigh less on other planets that have weaker gravity. For example, on Mars (a smaller planet than ours) your cake's weight would be less than half what it is on Earth. On Jupiter, which is the biggest planet in the Solar System, however, the cake would weigh 2.4 times more. Remember, though, that doesn't mean there is more cake! It just means that the cake is exerting a larger force because of increased gravity.

ALL MIXED UP

Even on Earth, weight changes with location. Gravity pulls from the middle of an object, and the Earth's poles are slightly closer to the core than the bulging sides around the equator. The result is that the Earth's pull is slightly stronger at the poles, so your weight increases a little. Similarly, your weight decreases a little as you climb to the top of a very high mountain.

It's the law!

Newton wasn't satisfied with just understanding gravity. He also explained how forces in general act upon objects, paving the way for a scientific revolution. His laws of motion (first published in 1687) form some of the most important basics of modern physics.

FIRST THINGS FIRST

Newton's first law says that objects cannot start moving, stop moving, or change direction by themselves unless a force acts on them. So, pushing a stationary skateboard makes it roll, and leaving it at the top of a slope allows gravity to pull it downward. A moving skateboard will slow down because of air resistance and friction between it and the floor. It will stop or swerve if you put your foot down as a brake, or if someone pushes you in the opposite direction.

Newton's explained his laws in *Philosophae Naturalis Principia Mathematica*, one of the most important science books ever written.

JUMPING TO THIRD

Newton's third law states that forces are found in pairs. He says that for every action (or force) there is an equal and opposite reaction (or force). If you are wearing rollerskates and you push against a wall, you move backward. Likewise, if you and a friend were both wearing rollerskates and you pushed against each other equally, you would both move in opposite directions.

LOOK OUT!

A SPORTING CHANCE

You can see all three laws in action in any sport. Kicking a ball adds the force it needs to move it (the first law). If it flies up in the air, gravity pulls it down (also the first law). If it hits the goalpost, it bounces back (the third law). If you kick it harder, it travels further. This is the second law, and it needs a bit more explaining. Read more on the next page ...

Just a second ...

So, you've read about Newton's first and third laws. What about the second law? Now we take into account another factor—the size of an object makes a difference to how it reacts to a force.

ACCELERATED LEARNING

Everyone knows that it is harder to stop a real truck than a toy truck. Newton's second law tells us that the bigger an object, the more force it takes to make it move or stop. It takes more force to accelerate a real truck than a toy truck, too. For most people, acceleration is an increase in speed. For scientists, acceleration is any change in speed or direction. Getting faster is positive acceleration, and slowing down is negative acceleration.

HOW BIG IS BIG?

You may have noticed that "bigger" is not a very accurate term. What is meant by bigger? Surely it takes more force to kick a football than to kick a balloon, even if the balloon is bigger than the ball? Scientifically, bigger means "has a greater mass," as explained on page 52. According to Newton's second law, the amount of force and the movement created are directly linked to the amount of mass being acted upon.

LAYING DOWN THE LAW

This third law also explains why a harder kick moves a football a greater distance than a soft kick moves the same ball. You are using more force to kick the same-sized object. Newton wrote this law as "F = ma", where "F" means force, "m" means mass, and "a" means acceleration. If you double the force, and the mass stays the same, you double the acceleration. These laws may seem very simple nowadays, but Newton's genius was in setting them out for all scientists to use.

Take the strain

The human body can only produce a limited amount of force on its own. However, we are clever enough to use simple machines such as levers and pulleys to increase the amount of force without increasing the amount of work or energy needed.

HEAVY LOADS

One of the simplest machines is a lever. It consists of a long bar resting on a base called a fulcrum or a pivot. By moving the pressure point further from the pivot, you can convert a small amount of force into a large force at the other end. A playground seesaw is a classic example. You can lift a much heavier person than yourself if you sit further away from the middle.

Many tools work by using a long handle to magnify the force. A hammer, bottle opener, wrench, and garden fork are all types of levers.

PUSH OR PULLEY?

Lifting a heavy item from low to high is tough. It requires a lot of force. Attaching it to a pulley reverses the direction of the force so you are pulling down instead of pushing up, and it feels easier. Winding your rope around two pulley wheels actually halves the amount of force you need, making it twice as easy. Add in two more pulley wheels to make it twice as easy again!

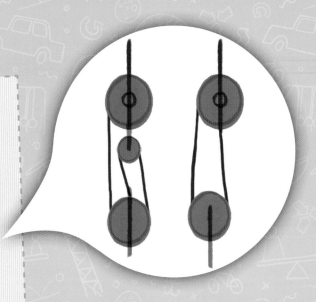

SUPER SCOOPER

No single person invented simple machines. Humans have developed tools since prehistoric times. However, Archimedes (287–212 BCE) is responsible for seeing the potential of one machine to do a new and vital job. He worked out how to use a rotating screw to lift water instead of having to pull it up in containers. The bottom of the screw scoops it up, and the water is carried up the screw as it turns.

Melted chocolate is lifted to the top level of a chocolate fountain by a rotating screw inside!

MYTH BUSTERS

Welcome to two things many people believe about forces, both of which are actually just a little bit ... wrong.

Newton wasn't hit by a falling apple!

Isaac Newton was an astonishing scientist. He changed the way we understand the universe. But did he really come up with his theory of gravity when an apple hit him on the head? Er ... no. His biographer, William Stukely, reports only that Newton saw an apple fall from a tree and began to wonder why objects always fell down, not to the side or upward. No geniuses were injured during the discovery.

STRANGE BUT TRUE!
Newton was born very prematurely, and his family was surprised that he survived.

There is gravity in space!

The Earth exerts gravity even at a distance, although in a reduced way. So an astronaut on the International Space Station (ISS) is not floating around because of a total lack of gravity. Instead, it is because the ISS, the equipment inside, and the astronaut are in a vacuum in space, with no air resistance to act against them. They are in a state known as free fall and are all being pulled toward Earth at the same speed. This state makes a pen, a person, or a huge piece of machinery fall together at the same speed, making things appear to float in relation to the space station.

YOUR BODY, EVERY BODY

The human body is one of the most astonishing machines on the planet. Scientists and medics are still amazed by how it works and what it can do, from healing itself to processing huge amounts of information at top speed.

Medical science looks at the way the body works, how to improve living conditions to make people more healthy, and how to cure diseases and fix things that are wrong. Great leaps in physics now allow doctors to see inside the body without harming it, using X-rays and scanning machines.

Before the 1850s, people believed that sickness was caused by breathing in poisonous fumes from decomposing waste, which they called "bad air." We now understand that specific germs cause specific diseases.

The first years

Humans are mammals, like cats, monkeys, and many other warm-blooded creatures. Like all other mammals, we grow inside our mother until we are developed enough to be born. Then we drink her milk to help us get bigger and stronger. Birds, reptiles, and fish usually lay eggs, and their babies eat live food even when they are still tiny.

SMALL BEGINNINGS

A person starts as a fertilized egg, which then divides to form a ball of cells, which lodges inside the mother's womb (uterus—a stretchy organ in her pelvis). It stays here for around 40 weeks, receiving oxygen and nutrients (food and water) from the mother's body. Most human babies are singletons, but about one in every seventy pregnancies are multiple births—twins, triplets, or even more!

The uterus is the size of a clenched fist to begin with, but stretches to the full size of the baby.

MAMMAL BABIES

Mammal babies develop at different rates. A human cannot walk until it is around a year old, but animals such as horses, cows, and antelope can walk within a few hours of being born. They might need to run away from predators! All mammal mothers produce milk for their babies to eat. Human milk is full of goodness, and a baby will triple its weight in its first year. That's nothing, though, compared to a blue whale calf, which gains 90 kg (200 lb) every day!

THE OUTSIDE WORLD

While your body is growing, so is your ability to fend for yourself. You learn how to walk and talk, recognize dangers, and retain information. A two-year-old's brain is already about 80% of its adult size, even though its body is only half of its adult height. The toddler's brain receives messages from the nervous system to keep it safe. These messages are sent from the eyes, nose, and ears, and from other sensory organs such as the skin and tastebuds.

Brain box

What's going on inside that head of yours? An awful lot! It is home to your brain, which is the main processing unit of your body's whole nervous system. It controls a huge number of things, including your movements, emotions, memories, appetite, and body temperature.

The human brain changes throughout childhood. Many neurons are lost as the adult brain develops.

HEART OR HEAD?

The Ancient Egyptians believed that thoughts and intelligence came from the heart, not the brain. The Ancient Greeks were probably the first to study the "mind" that rules our senses and actions. It was only in the nineteenth century that scientists working on animal brains worked out that nerves carried electrical pulses, and early neuroscience was born. The French surgeon Paul Broca (1824–1880) demonstrated that specific parts of the brain ruled different functions such as language and memory.

INSIDE YOUR MIND

The human body contains billions of nerve cells called neurons that zap messages around from the brain to the body and from the body to the brain. They are too minuscule to see with the naked eye, but under a microscope these neurons look like strange alien creatures. They send tiny electrical signals to each other, to tell your brain if your body is too hot or cold, if danger may be present, or if you are hungry or tired. They also relay messages back to your muscles, making your legs move and managing your digestive system.

MIND MAP

Different sections of the brain handle aspects such as emotions, memory, balance, the ability to plan ahead and solve problems, and what your senses are telling you about the world around you.

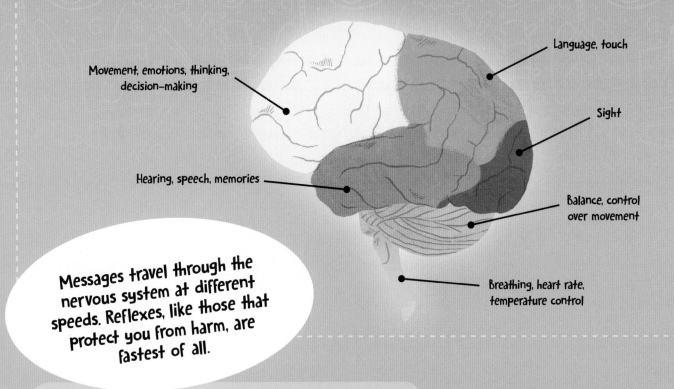

Movement, emotions, thinking, decision-making

Language, touch

Sight

Hearing, speech, memories

Balance, control over movement

Breathing, heart rate, temperature control

Messages travel through the nervous system at different speeds. Reflexes, like those that protect you from harm, are fastest of all.

BRAIN PICTURES

The different areas of the brain interact in amazing ways to keep your body functioning. Scientists can study which areas of the brain are used for different tasks by measuring the electrical activity on an EEG (electroencephalogram) scan. It can also help them diagnose conditions such as epilepsy and dementia.

Under attack!

Your brilliant body is not indestructible. It can be damaged in an accident, or become diseased. Some diseases start within the body and are called non-infectious. Many other diseases come from the outside and are caused by nasty things we often call germs.

BECOMING SICK

Germs can get inside the body in various ways. Some invade an open wound or are spread by contact with a person who already has the infection. Often, we become ill because we have breathed in germs, or swallowed them with food or water. Other illnesses are passed on by germ-carrying creatures. Mosquitoes spread over 100 diseases that affect around 700 million humans every year, and kill more than a million people.

The "Black Death" killed at least one-third of the population of Europe in the 1300s. It was a bacterial disease spread by rats.

GERMS ON DISPLAY

There are four main types of germs—bacteria, viruses, fungi, and protozoa. All of them are tiny living creatures that live by getting nutrients from plants and animals. Two of them, bacteria and viruses, cause a vast number of diseases and infections, from sore throats and toothache to flu and measles. Viruses can only survive inside living cells and cannot be killed off with medicine. Bacteria can reproduce on their own, and are often treated with antibiotics.

DIRTY DISEASES

Fungi and protozoa can make people uncomfortable or very ill. Fungi love damp, warm places and often cause itchy rashes such as athlete's foot or ringworm. Protozoa are carried by insects or thrive in dirty water, leading to stomachaches, sickness, and diarrhea. These diseases are especially common in developing countries, where clean water is unavailable for drinking and bathing. Nearly 1 billion people around the world do not have access to safe, clean drinking water.

Louis Pasteur's discovery that germs cause disease led to the development of antiseptics and vaccinations, and has saved countless millions of lives.

Facing the enemy

Doctors can give you medicine to treat illness, but your body has its own way of fighting off many types of germ. Your immune system is a network of cells, tissues, and organs that work together to defend the body against attack by "foreign" invaders.

MEGA MONSTERS

Human blood contains two types of white cells, phagocytes and lymphocytes, which fight off invaders. Phagocytes are warriors that surround invading organisms. They either engulf (swallow up) these organisms to get rid of them, or inject them with an enzyme which destroys them. Russian zoologist Ilya Mechnikov (1845–1916) discovered phagocytes in 1882 while he was studying starfish! He won the 1908 Nobel Prize for his contribution to studies in human immunity.

Washing your hands can stop some bacteria from getting into your body, but once they're inside, you'll need your white blood cells to fight them off!

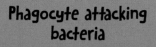

Phagocyte attacking bacteria

MEMORY TEST

Lymphocyte

The second type of white blood cells, lymphocytes, are tactical soldiers. They carry chemicals called antibodies, which lock on to the invaders and stick to them to damage or destroy them. They can also send signals to phagocytes to call them to action. The lymphocytes remember previous invaders to help the body deal with them efficiently. That is why you are better able to fight off an illness if your body has got rid of it previously.

One pint of human blood contains over three billion phagocytes.

WIPING OUT DISEASE

In 1798, a doctor named Edward Jenner showed how a weakened form of a disease could be used to fight off a full-strength version. He inserted germs into the body (notably of his own baby son!) to demonstrate that it built up immunity. Louis Pasteur (1822–1895) used Jenner's findings many years later. He injected farm animals with his new anthrax vaccine. When exposed to a deadly dose of anthrax, all of them survived. Today, many life-threatening human diseases have been brought under control by vaccinating people around the world.

Smallpox has been eradicated (completely wiped out) worldwide thanks to vaccinations.

Organ recital

It is easy to see what's on your outside—skin, nails, hair, eyes, and mouth. But the hidden workings of the body are harder to study. Doctors are still learning about how the insides work, from brain cells to the vital organs and the systems they make up.

GROUND-BREAKING

The Ancient Egyptians knew plenty about body parts, as they removed organs to mummify their dead. Over the following centuries, great thinkers found out more about the vessels that carry blood (Aristotle described arteries and veins in the fourth century BCE), how the skeleton and muscles work (Belgian physician Andreas Vesalius was nicknamed the Father of Anatomy for his human body book published in 1543), and even how to transplant an organ from one person to another.

Brain

Lungs

Heart

Stomach

Liver

Small intestine

Large intestine

ALL SYSTEMS ARE GO

The organs of the body work together as systems. The heart (left) is the driving force in the circulatory system, moving blood around. The lungs (below) are part of the respiratory system that allows us to breathe. The skeleton and muscles link up so we can move and function. Our digestive system obtains and delivers nutrients, and our urinary system gets rid of the waste. Many organs fit into more than one system and do multiple jobs.

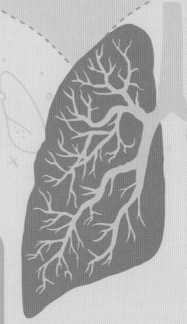

The first human heart transplant was carried out by South African surgeon Christiaan Barnard in 1967.

WORKING HARD

Your heart pumps non-stop, 24-7, pushing blood to the very tips of your toes. It ensures that every cell in your body receives oxygen and nutrients. In fact, the average human heart beats more than 100,000 times per day. The liver is also extremely busy. It's the largest internal organ, just below your rib cage, and it does more than 500 jobs. Without it, your blood would not clot, you would be vulnerable to toxins, and you wouldn't be able to digest food or go to the toilet.

Close to the bone

Bones are tough, and protect your softer organs as well as keeping you strong and upright so you can move around. It was once thought that they were made of earth, as they were so cold and dry. Even these sturdy structures can be damaged and broken, though.

LAYER UPON LAYER

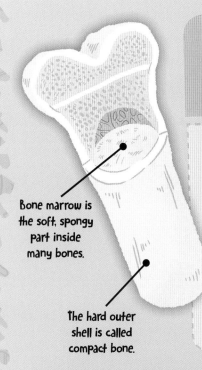

Bone marrow is the soft, spongy part inside many bones.

The hard outer shell is called compact bone.

Bones are not the dry, dead objects that you might think of at Halloween. They are living things that can grow and heal. The smooth, hard surface that you see on a skeleton model is covered by a thin outer layer of nerves and blood vessels. Inside, there is a spongy layer that keeps your bones strong but lightweight. Some bones have bone marrow inside, where new blood cells are made.

BENDY BITS

Your bones need other body parts to hold them together and make them move. Cartilage acts as a cushion between bones so they don't rub together and wear out. Strong, stretchy tissues called ligaments and tendons join your bones and muscles together. The longest tendon is the plantaris, which runs down the back of the lower leg. It can cause pain in young people when they grow especially fast.

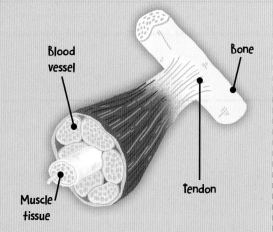

Blood vessel

Bone

Muscle tissue

Tendon

WHERE BONES MEET

Bones are rigid and tough. They can't bend, so you can only move your body at a point where your bones meet. This place is called a synovial joint. These are some of the joints in your body.

Your hip joint is a ball and socket joint that lets you move your leg in many directions.

Your knee joint is a hinge joint that lets you move your leg backward and forward.

The joints in your hand are gliding joints that let the bones slide over one another back and forth or side to side.

A pivot joint is found between your top two vertebrae, just under the skull. It lets you turn your head from side to side.

LOOKING INSIDE

An accident can fracture (break) a bone into two or more pieces. The human body is so incredible that it instantly begins to heal itself. New bone forms in the break to join the pieces together. An X-ray helps medical staff see inside the body to look at the damage. This amazing invention was introduced in the Balkan War in 1897, after German scientist Wilhelm Röntgen discovered that the light rays could be used to see through flesh and form a photograph of the bones inside.

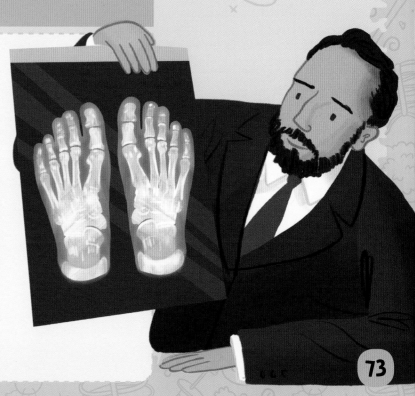

Mega muscles

There is more muscle tissue in the human body than any other kind of tissue. Muscles help you move, from large leaps to tiny blinks of your eye. Many hidden muscles do vital jobs, helping food travel through the digestive system and pushing out waste at the other end.

Humans have six muscles to move their ears, in contrast to super-sensitive cats, which have 32 for each ear.

BEAUTIFUL TO BEHOLD

People have more than 600 skeletal muscles. These are the ones that control voluntary movements, helping you sit and stand, jump and run, and nod and smile. Muscles are easier to see than many body parts. Many early artists were fascinated by the human form and produced countless drawings of human anatomy and muscles. The Roman anatomist Galen studied the wounds of gladiators to find out all he could about the human body.

BEND AND STRETCH

Skeletal muscles are attached to bones by tendons. Muscles often work in pairs to move your bones. A muscle cannot push, it can only pull. So as one muscle pulls a limb into place (such as bending your arm at the elbow), its opposite muscle is needed to pull in the other direction to make the arm straight again. Each time, the muscle contracts (gets shorter) to perform the pulling action, and then relaxes (gets longer) to release the movement.

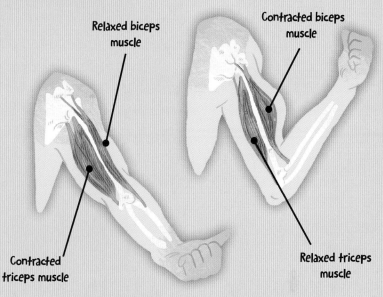

Relaxed biceps muscle

Contracted biceps muscle

Contracted triceps muscle

Relaxed triceps muscle

SUPER SMOOTH

The hidden muscles are found deep inside your organs, and work on their own without you thinking about it. They are called smooth muscles, and make the walls of your organs contract in waves. These waves help to move things along, pushing food through the intestines, blood through your veins and arteries, urine out of your bladder, and your food through your stomach and intestines. Skeletal muscles get tired relatively quickly, smooth muscles don't get tired very often, and cardiac (heart) muscles never, ever get tired!

Chomp!

Smooth muscle

Touchy feely

Your senses make you aware of what's happening around you. Your eyes, ears, nose, mouth, and skin pass messages from the outside world along your nervous system to your brain, so your body can react and keep you safe. They also contribute to your emotions, giving pleasure as well as warnings.

Your nose picks up smells as you breathe in.

SENSITIVE SUBJECT

Your skin is the largest organ in your body. It allows you to feel your way through life, picking up messages about heat, pressure, and pain. Tiny hairs and touch receptors tell your brain if you have an itch, are being tickled, are walking on soft grass or rough stones, and whether you are in contact with something hot, cold, or sharp. Some areas have more receptors and so are more sensitive than others.

Ears pick up sounds and tell you what you're hearing.

Your sense of sight gives you a picture of the world around you.

Is it sweet or salty? Taste buds on your tongue tell you how food tastes.

Your sense of touch tells you how things feel.

LOOK OUT!

The eyes pick up light signals and the ears collect sound waves. These are translated in the brain into what you can see and hear. Smells are detected in your nose, and add to the sensations passed on by your taste buds to let you know if something is appealing and tasty or unappealing and might harm you. Humans rely heavily on their sight. The eyes contribute around 80 percent of what you learn, and can handle over 30,000 pieces of information in an hour.

The back is the least sensitive part of the body, and the lips, tongue and fingertips have the most touch receptors.

EXTRA SENSORY

Modern science says that these five senses are not all we have. Other abilities can also be classed as senses, such as "equilibrioception," which is the ability to keep your balance and change direction, and "proprioception," which lets you know where your body parts are in relation to each other. This sense is what lets you scratch an itch on your back without being able to see it, or point to your nose with your eyes closed.

MYTH BUSTERS

What common beliefs can we blow out of the water this time? Do our bodies really behave the way we think they do? Most probably not.

We use our <u>whole</u> brain!

People sometimes say that we only use 10% of our brain, and that if only we could harness more of our brainpower, homework would be a piece of cake and tests wouldn't be a challenge! However, this statistic is based on folklore, not fact. Studies of the brain show that all areas have a role to play, and most of them are active most of the time. Some might take a break depending on the task you're doing, but certain sections keep on firing even when you sleep. It seems that the main limit on your own brainpower is how you choose to use it.

Carrots <u>don't</u> help you see in the dark!

Your grandparents might roll this one out to persuade you to eat your veggies, but no amount of carrot crunching will give you night goggles. It is true enough that the vitamin A in carrots is essential for healthy eyes. But eating more of it does not make you see better, beyond a certain limit. It certainly doesn't allow you to see in total darkness!

HIGH ENERGY

Energy exists in lots of different forms. The two main types are potential energy (which is stored in objects) and kinetic energy, in moving things. Your body uses stored energy from food and changes it into kinetic energy so you can run around.

Kinetic energy can be converted into other useful energy forms—heat, light, sound, and electrical energy. Chemical, mechanical, gravitational, and nuclear energy are all potential energy, and can be transformed into electricity (for example, at a power station).

Scientists define energy as "the ability to do work." Sometimes we use energy for fun and play, though—which hardly feels like work!

Feel the heat

The Sun warms the Earth, the stove warms your soup, a cup of hot chocolate warms your hands ... toasty! Heat is the transfer of thermal energy and happens in different ways depending upon the substances involved. Scientists call these ways conduction, convection, and radiation.

MOVE ALONG, PLEASE

Conduction takes place in solids. As one particle (speck of matter) gets heated, it begins to move and shake more quickly. Some of the heat energy is passed to the particles around it, until eventually all of the particles are hotter. Metals pass heat along easily; they are good conductors. Gases such as air and non-metals such as plastic and wool are poor conductors. That's why metal saucepans have plastic handles, so they don't burn you when you lift them.

If two touching objects have two different temperatures, heat will always move from the warmer object to the cooler one. For example, heat goes from a stovetop to the bottom of a pan.

ONWARD AND UPWARD

Convection is the transfer of thermal energy in liquids and gases, and it takes place naturally in the oceans, in the atmosphere, and in the magma in the Earth's layers. The heat moves from hot places to cooler places within the liquid, forming a current. Particles with lots of heat energy move upward and take the place of particles with less heat energy. These cooler particles move down, creating a circular motion. This is how soup heats in a pan, and how a hot air balloon stays aloft.

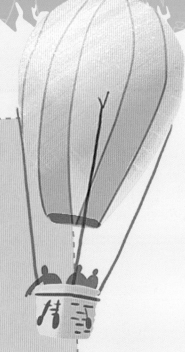

TAKING UP SPACE

The particles in liquids and gases are not bound together like those in solids. They are free to move around and occupy whatever room is allowed by the container holding them. When they are heated, the particles move more and the gaps between them get bigger. They expand and become less dense, making them rise. The cooler particles are still dense, so they sink. This is why on a hot day, the upstairs of a house might be even hotter than the downstairs!

Natural convection in the air causes wind, when hot air rises and cool air rushes in.

Heat wave!

There is no air in space to allow conduction or convection. So how does the Sun's warmth reach us? It is transferred by radiation, which uses infrared waves, rather than particles, to carry heat.

HOT STUFF

The same thing happens on a smaller scale when the air is heated around a lightbulb or an open fire. The hotter an object is, the more infrared radiation it gives off. Pale, shiny surfaces reflect radiation, and dark, dull surfaces are better at absorbing and emitting radiation. Infrared panels are used on the ISS to collect heat in space, while the body of the station is covered in shiny silver mesh to keep out radiation and protect the astronauts and their equipment.

Infrared waves are used in a remote control to change the channel on your TV.

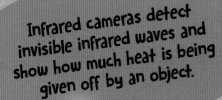

Infrared cameras detect invisible infrared waves and show how much heat is being given off by an object.

GIVE US A WAVE

Infrared waves are similar to light waves (see page 88), but they are felt as heat rather than seen as light. They were discovered in 1800 by the astronomer William Herschel. By passing light through a prism, he split light into a rainbow and recorded the temperature of the different shades. He found that the temperature increased from blue up to red and was even higher beyond the red, where no light was visible. He called it infrared.

ROMAN RADIATION

The Ancient Romans knew about the different types of heat transfer. They developed hypocausts, where air was heated by a fire, then circulated under a raised floor and through hollow walls to warm the rooms of a building. This system used radiation, convection, and conduction to heat their properties, especially the public baths that were popular in Roman times.

Science degrees

On a hot day, it gets warmer and the temperature rises. In winter, it gets colder and the temperature might drop below zero degrees. But what does "temperature" actually mean?

ENERGY FLOW

Heat and temperature are related but are not the same. Heat is the flow of energy from one object to another, while temperature is the degree or strength of the heat. This energy is called heat energy, caused by the bumping together of particles (see page 89). The amount of energy contained in an object is measured in joules. The unit is named after James Joule (1784–1858), who studied heat and the transfer of energy, and has a thermodynamic law named after him.

Energy can be measured in calories as well as joules. the calorie rating given to food is how much energy it contains.

MEASURE FOR MEASURE

Early temperature-measuring devices called thermoscopes existed in the 1600s. They showed changes in temperature but had no standard scale for comparing numbers between devices. In 1724 a German physicist named Daniel Gabriel Fahrenheit (1686–1736) made a scale that had 180 degrees between melting ice and boiling water. Later that century, the Swedish astronomer Anders Celsius (pictured, right) proposed a scale with just 100 degrees difference (although it was the opposite to what we know now, with water boiling at 0 degrees and water freezing at 100 degrees).

The two scales coincide at just one temperature— minus 40 degrees Fahrenheit is also minus 40 degrees Celsius.

HOW HOT?

Temperature tells us how hot or cold something is, and is measured in degrees (Celsius, Fahrenheit, or a third system, Kelvin). If heat energy is transferred to an object, its temperature rises. However, something with a lot of heat energy can still have a lower temperature than something with less heat energy. A swimming pool is clearly much cooler than a kettle of boiling water. However, the pool contains a lot more water, so it stores more heat energy than the small kettle.

Sounding off

Sound is a wave that is created by vibrations, and moves from one place to another through a solid, liquid, or gas. Sound cannot travel through space, as it needs particles to carry it. It So, if a movie about space is full of explosions and whooshing noises, it's actually misleading you!

GOOD VIBRATIONS

Sound begins as a vibration caused by movements. Any movement can make a sound—a spoon hitting the floor, a dog barking, a plane passing overhead. The stronger the vibrations, the louder the sound. In 1660, Robert Boyle (1627-1691) proved that sound needs something to carry it. He put a ringing bell inside a glass jar and sucked out the air with a pump. The sound died out as the air disappeared.

Sound travels faster through water than through air, as the liquid particles are closer together as they transfer the sound waves.

EAR WE GO

The vibrating object forces the air around it to vibrate, carrying the energy with it on waves. When these waves reach your ear, they make the eardrum inside your ear vibrate. This moves tiny bones called ossicles, which in turn vibrate a liquid further inside your head, in the cochlea. The liquid causes movement in minuscule hairs to create nerve signals. The hearing nerve sends these messages to your brain, which translates them so you know what you are listening to.

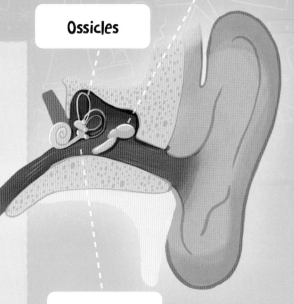

Eardrum

Ossicles

Cochlea

High-frequency sounds (above 20,000Hz) are called ultrasounds. They can be used to make images to see inside the human body.

HIGH AND LOW

The frequency of sound waves is measured in Hertz, named after Heinrich Hertz (1857–1894), a German physicist who discovered radio waves in 1886. A measurement of 20Hz means that 20 waves hit our ears every second. Humans can generally hear sounds in the range of 20–20,000Hz. If a sound's frequency is too low or high, we cannot hear it. Many animals can, though. Dogs hear up to 60,000Hz, and bats and dolphins can hear sounds over 100,000Hz.

The speed of light

Light travels at different speeds when it passes through anything other than a vacuum. The light waves bounce off any particles they meet in the air, or in liquids and solids such as water and glass. In a vacuum, there are no particles to slow light down.

FLASHLIGHTS

It was once thought that the speed of light was too fast to measure. Galileo (right) disagreed, and was determined to find out how fast it went. He experimented in 1638 by standing a measured distance from his assistant and timing the interval between lighting a lantern and seeing his assistant flash another light to show he had seen it. It was too small a time gap for Galileo to measure.

According to different accounts, Galileo attempted to time light speed using his pulse or a water clock.

SUPER SPEED

Nearly 40 years later, the Danish astronomer Ole Rømer (1644–1710) calculated the speed of light by accident. He noticed that the timing of eclipses of Jupiter's moons differed by several minutes, and figured that it was due to the time it takes for light to travel from Jupiter to Earth. His measurements have since been refined, and we now know that the speed of light in a vacuum is 299,792,458 m/s (186,282 miles/sec). That would take you around the world about 7½ times in one second!

Rømer also played a part in the invention of the thermometer, making a temperature scale that was the basis of Fahrenheit's later work.

BENDING LIGHT

Light travels slower through materials with more particles. These materials are said to be "optically dense." As light passes between materials of different density, it changes speed. This makes it bend off course (known as refraction) and causes some spectacular visual effects. It can make a pencil sticking out of a glass of water look bent. Refraction is also what makes stars twinkle in the night sky.

Sparky stuff

Electricity is the form of energy you are probably most familiar with. It is a kind of kinetic energy, and can be converted to heat and light energy to use in our homes, or to power video games and charge your phone. If you had lived before World War I, you would only have had electricity in your home if you were very rich. Imagine that!

EARLY SPARKS

No one invented electricity, as it occurs naturally. It was first recognized in ancient times in the form of static electricity. In around 500 BCE Thales of Miletus showed that rubbing two things together, such as fur on amber, caused an attraction between them. This is static electricity. It was many centuries before people worked out how electricity could move as a current.

STRIKING OUT

Some of the greatest names in science carried out experiments with electricity. Benjamin Franklin (1706–1790) proved, in 1752, that lightning was static electricity. In 1800 Alessandro Volta (left, 1745–1827) discovered that certain chemical reactions produced electricity. He invented the voltaic pile, consisting of a stack of metal discs with wet cardboard discs in between. It was the first electric battery, and it was a breakthrough in creating continuous electric current.

In 1836, Faraday invented a cage that can block out electric charges by spreading them around a metal mesh.

LIGHTBULB MOMENTS

Michael Faraday (right, 1791–1867) used a magnet to generate electric current in 1831. He showed that magnets and electricity are linked and can be used to make things move. Scientists also investigated how electricity could be converted to light. At least two people (most famously, Thomas Edison and James Swan) are credited with inventing the lightbulb. Thomas Edison took his invention to the next stage by setting up the system needed to supply electricity to power the bulb in the streets of New York, and later in buildings.

Splitting the atom

All matter in the universe is made of very tiny building blocks called atoms. An element (such as helium or gold) is made up of only one type of atom. A compound (such as water) is made up of more than one type of atom. In the twentieth century, scientists began to find out what makes up the atoms.

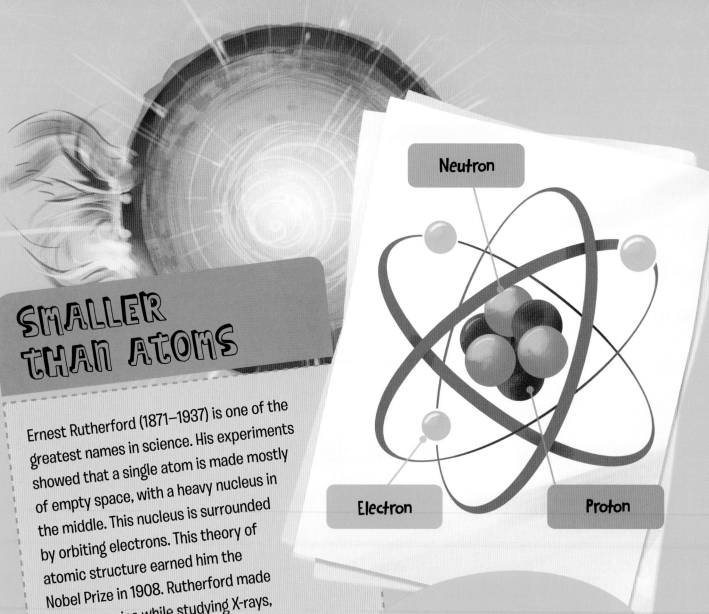

Neutron

Electron

Proton

SMALLER THAN ATOMS

Ernest Rutherford (1871–1937) is one of the greatest names in science. His experiments showed that a single atom is made mostly of empty space, with a heavy nucleus in the middle. This nucleus is surrounded by orbiting electrons. This theory of atomic structure earned him the Nobel Prize in 1908. Rutherford made his discoveries while studying X-rays, identified in 1895 by Wilhelm Röntgen.

The nucleus in the middle is composed of protons and neutrons. Zooming around the nucleus (like the Moon orbiting the Earth!) are electrons.

BREAKING DOWN

Some atoms have an unstable nucleus, allowing them to split up and give off radiation. Rutherford tested radioactive elements and found two different types of radiation, alpha and beta. A third type, gamma radiation, was identified by Henri Becquerel. His name is given to the unit of nuclear activity, which tells us how many nuclei give off radiation per second. The first four radioactive elements (uranium, thorium, radium, and polonium) were documented or discovered by Marie Curie and her husband Pierre.

DANGER ZONE

Radiation can be extremely dangerous to humans. It affects the body's cells and can cause cancer or kill you. Unfortunately, radiation cannot be seen, smelled, or touched, so how do we tell it's there? We use a detector, called a Geiger counter or Geiger–Müller tube, which gives off clicks if it absorbs radiation. The more rapid the rate of clicks, the higher the radiation levels are. It was invented by one of Rutherford's team of nuclear physicists, Hans Geiger.

The concept of radioactivity was discovered by Henri Becquerel in 1896, but the name "radioactivity" was made up by Marie Curie in 1898.

Radioactive risks

When radiation was discovered, scientists believed that it could be used to target many different types of disease. New medicines and products were developed, but the deaths of patients and factory workers in the 1920s and 1930s raised concerns. Now we understand that the same therapy that kills cancer cells will also damage healthy cells.

FEEL THE GLOW

When radioactivity was explained to the world, it was poorly understood by non-scientists. Businesses looking to make easy money added radioactive thorium and radium to toothpaste and cosmetics, claiming they could brighten and rejuvenate teeth and skin. Nowadays we know that exposure to too much radiation can damage living tissue and cause cancer. Even medical X-rays, which give off radiation, can make doctors and nurses sick if they are exposed to them too often.

In the early twentieth century, several toothpastes had radioactive ingredients for extra whiteness. Other radioactive products included lipsticks, cigarettes, and even chocolate bars!

DAMAGE AND DESTRUCTION

The three types of radiation affect humans in different ways. Beta particles and gamma rays are the most dangerous if they come from an outside source, as they can penetrate the skin and get to cells inside. However, if swallowed or breathed in, alpha radiation causes the most damage, as it is easily absorbed by cells inside the body.

A LONG-LASTING LEGACY

Even the scientists carrying out early investigations were unaware of the dangers of radioactivity. Marie Curie's extensive studies took a toll on her health, and years of exposure to radiation led to her early death in 1934. She was said to carry test tubes of radioactive elements in her pockets, and kept one by her bed to glow as a nightlight! Her notebooks are so radioactive they still cannot safely be studied, and her body was buried in a lead-lined coffin to prevent the radiation from leaking out.

Marie Curie was the first woman in history to win a Nobel Prize, and the first person (man or woman) to win the award twice.

MYTH BUSTERS

What do you know about this pair of scientific greats? The chances are that you have heard two of the most widely spread myths in the history of science.

Franklin (probably) <u>didn't</u> get struck by lightning!

The American inventor Benjamin Franklin was fascinated by electricity. He believed that it was linked to lightning, and is said to have proved it by sending up a kite in a thunderstorm to try to collect sparks. It is a very famous story, but it might not be true. Franklin may only have reported on someone else's experiment. Certainly, the kite was not struck by lightning or it would have killed him. More likely, it picked up small amounts of electrical charge from the air.

Einstein <u>wasn't</u> a failure at school!

Einstein is commonly used as an example of someone who struggled at school but showed his genius in adult life. It is true that he was a daydreamer, and objected to the strict teaching methods, but by the age of 11 he was reading college books on physics. Not so stupid! He did fail the entrance exam to college, but probably because it was in French, Einstein's second language. And he was taking it aged only 16, before he had even graduated from high school!

GETTING A
REACTION

If you're looking for the kind of science that goes "BOOM!" then this is the place for you. Chemists look at reactions between materials, researching and describing what happens when substances are mixed together or broken apart.

Physicists also like their fair share of explosions, and sometimes on a grand scale. They study some really big questions, such as how the universe began? At the opposite extreme, physicists look at the very smallest breakdown of particles to see how atoms work. Splitting and joining these atoms has led to some of the biggest bangs in history— from the birth of the Sun to the creation of nuclear bombs.

Everlasting life

Early scientists observed the world around them and made their best guesses about what made things happen. Many of them were alchemists, looking for the secret of living forever. Many experiments, investigations, and discoveries made in recent centuries have their roots in this early branch of science.

Alchemists believed that all matter was made up of four elements—earth, air, fire, and water.

MAKING MAGIC

Alchemists were trying to find an elixir of life, to bring them riches, wisdom, and the possibility of eternal life. They also searched for "the philosopher's stone," a substance that could turn base (common) metals into precious ones such as gold. They experimented on rocks and minerals, trying to purify them and transform them. Their notes used symbols from astrology, myths, and religion, making them look more like spell books than textbooks.

ELEMENT OF SURPRISE

In 1669, a German named Hennig Brand (1630–unknown) believed that he could turn urine into gold. He collected gallons of it and began a lengthy process to boil and distill it. It did not produce gold, but he did notice that the substance he was left with gave off a green glow. He had collected phosphorous, now used in fertilizer, detergents, and matches. It was the first element to be discovered since ancient times.

two of science's most influential figures—Robert Boyle and Isaac Newton—were interested in alchemy.

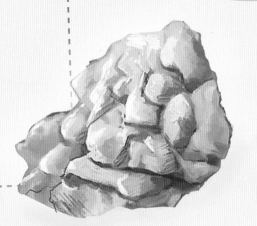

BACK TO THE FUTURE

Alchemy has played an important role in modern science. It led to the "scientific method" of collecting data in a controlled way, and testing for different outcomes. Robert Boyle (1627–1691) was notable for his logical methodology and recording of notes and results. He is often regarded as a founder of modern chemistry. Another early alchemist, Maria the Jewess (*circa* first century CE), perfected the process of distillation and introduced the use of glass containers, still used today, so that changes could be observed during experiments.

Made in Space

When the universe first began to form after the "Big Bang" around 14 billion years ago, the only elements were the lightest ones—mostly hydrogen and helium, with tiny amounts of lithium and beryllium. Nuclear reactions in newly formed stars and giant supernovae (exploding stars) began to create new, heavier elements.

WHAT IS AN ELEMENT?

An element is a pure substance that cannot be broken down into anything else. Every particle in it is the same. These particles are called atoms. People have known about many metallic elements (copper, lead, iron, gold, and silver) for thousands of years. Chemists in the 1700s identified lots of new elements, including the gases hydrogen, nitrogen, and oxygen. Several new elements were created in laboratories at the end of the twentieth century.

New elements are often named after famous scientists, such as nobelium, rutherfordium, and roentgenium.

BUILDING BLOCKS

You, like all things, are made of elements. Your body mostly consists of carbon, oxygen, and hydrogen, plus much smaller amounts of calcium and phosphorus in your teeth and bones, and nitrogen, which helps with making proteins and repairing cells. These elements were all created in the star reactions at the beginning of time—so the basic building blocks of your body are billions of years old.

INGREDIENTS FOR LIFE

Elements can combine to form new substances called compounds. Oxygen and hydrogen, for example, can be chemically joined to make water. Scientists have a formula for writing this, using symbols for each element. Water is shown as H_2O, as it is two parts hydrogen to one part oxygen. Carbon dioxide, which you breathe out all the time, is CO_2 (one carbon atom and two oxygen atoms). Other compounds are found in everyday life—for example, sodium and chlorine form table salt, or sodium chloride ($NaCl$).

Elementary

There are 94 naturally occurring elements, plus 24 others that are not found naturally on Earth. They have been created in laboratory conditions. Some of these synthetic elements (made artificially) exist for only a split second before they decay and turn into other elements.

IN THE LAB

All man-made elements are radioactive. They release particles and become lighter elements. The first to be created was curium, made in 1944 by scientists bombarding plutonium with other particles to break it down. Plutonium is a silvery metal that was itself created by blasting uranium (a naturally occurring radioactive element), and it has since been found in small amounts in the Earth's crust. Cyclotrons (right) and modern synchotrons are large machines that can be used to accelerate particles and create new elements.

THE BIGGER PICTURE

The most common elements in the universe are hydrogen (74%) and helium (around 24%) although these numbers are scientists' best-guesses. They can't be entirely sure what is out there on such a grand scale. In our own atmosphere, nitrogen makes up the largest part (roughly 78%), and then oxygen (nearly 21%). Both of these elements are vital for life on Earth—nitrogen for building body tissues and oxygen for burning fuel in our bodies to give us energy.

The discovery of plutonium was kept a secret until after the end of World War II, as it can be used to make nuclear weapons.

LIFE ON EARTH

The most common element within Earth's crust is oxygen, followed by silicon (found in tough rocks such as granite). That's handy, as silicon has many uses, from the computer chip that allows your phone to be so small but powerful, to the billions of tons of glass used in buildings around the world. Silicon aroused little interest with early scientists, and was only properly discovered as an element in 1824.

Periodic patterns

More than 50 elements had been discovered by the 1860s. Scientists began to notice patterns, and started to arrange them by their properties. They tried different ways of grouping them in an attempt to make more sense of the elemental world. The first to try was the German Johann Döbereiner in 1817.

PRIME PROPERTY

Döbereiner (1780–1849) sorted the elements into sets of three, according to their relative atomic mass (how heavy an atom is compared to a carbon atom). This highlighted patterns in their properties, such as whether the element was a metal or a non-metal and how hard or dense it is. Other properties include an element's reactivity, its melting point, how well it burns or bends, and whether it conducts electricity or heat. Chemistry is the science that studies the structure and properties of substances and the changes that they go through.

In 1808, Sir Humphrey Davy discovered an element that he called "aluminum." The name was later changed in some parts of the world to follow the –ium pattern of other elements, such as sodium and magnesium.

CHEMICAL CARD GAME

English scientist John Newlands (1837–1898) also used relative atomic mass to group the elements in 1864, but he put them into octaves (groups of eight). Then in 1869 the Russian Dmitri Mendeleev (1834–1907) (right) had a breakthrough. Allegedly, his love of the card game solitaire led him to lay out cards featuring all the known elements (63 by this time) in increasing order of their atomic weights. He placed them in rows and columns, just like the card game.

DON'T MIND THE GAP

Mendeleev's genius was that where his arrangement left gaps, he wasn't worried. He figured that those elements were still waiting to be discovered. His newly named "periodic table" allowed him to work out the atomic mass of the missing elements, and predict their properties. He predicted, for example, that something should sit in row 4 of group 13, and he even predicted many of the details that the element would have. In 1875 (6 years later), gallium was discovered and filled the gap.

Mixing it up

Elements cannot be broken down into simpler substances, but they can be joined together to make other substances called compounds. Compounds only form when elements react. They cannot just be mixed together in a container; they have to swap or share particles and form new chemical bonds.

SLOW OR SPECTACULAR?

Some reactions take place slowly. Iron reacts with water and oxygen to form rust, for example. This happens when you leave your bike out in the rain, but it won't go rusty overnight. Some reactions are very fast, however, such as mixing vinegar and baking soda to make it foam and froth. Two reactions happen here—hydrogen in the vinegar reacts with sodium and bicarbonate to create carbonic acid, which immediately begins to decompose into water and carbon dioxide gas, forming bubbles.

Alkali metals such as lithium, sodium, and potassium are so reactive they are stored in oil to stop them reacting with air.

HUMAN REACTIONS

Reactions need a certain amount of energy to take place. Usually, this is in the form of heat energy. Blacksmiths have known this for centuries, as they mix different metals together at high temperatures to make weapons with the strengths of different elements. A reaction may occur faster by using a catalyst (a substance that alters the way a reaction happens, without being changed itself). Your body uses catalysts (called enzymes) to help break down food into usable energy for your muscles.

NOTHING TO SEE HERE

Some elements don't react easily, or at all. These include the metals gold and platinum, and a column of non-reactive gases at the far right of the periodic table. These gases (helium, neon, argon, krypton, xenon, and radon) were discovered between 1894 and 1898 by Scottish chemist Sir William Ramsey (1852–1916). They form their own group in the periodic table, named noble gases.

Noble gases are useful because of their unreactivity. Helium replaced hydrogen in airships, as it does not explode but is still less dense than air, so it makes the airships float.

Swap and share

Elements react because they have particles called electrons spinning around their central nucleus. These electrons can move around to form bonds. An element's reactivity depends on the number and arrangement of its electrons. Elements lower down their group in the periodic table are more reactive than those above them.

INSIDE THE ATOM

In 1897, an English physicist named J.J. Thomson (1856–1940) was studying rays of particles in a glass tube called a cathode ray tube. The actions of the particles led him to propose that all atoms are made of positively and negatively charged particles. He didn't get it exactly right; he thought they were dotted here, there and everywhere, like blueberries in a muffin. In reality, their positions are more regular.

Thomson had discovered electrons, although he originally called them "corpuscles." He proved that the atom was not the smallest unit, as had been thought previously.

A POSITIVE RESULT

New Zealand-born physicist Ernest Rutherford (1871–1937) was intrigued by these subatomic particles. He carried out more experiments and eventually came up with a model of an atom that had a central, positively charged nucleus with negative electrons floating around it. The Danish physicist Niels Bohr (1885–1962) refined this, saying that the electrons were in fixed orbits, like the planets around the Sun.

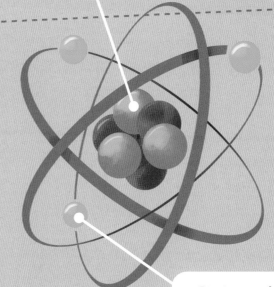

The nucleus is made up of positively charged protons and chargeless neutrons.

Electrons, which have a negative charge, orbit the nucleus.

The work of Thomson, Rutherford, and Bohr was so important that all three of them were awarded the Nobel Prize (in 1906, 1908, and 1922 respectively).

BONDING SESSION

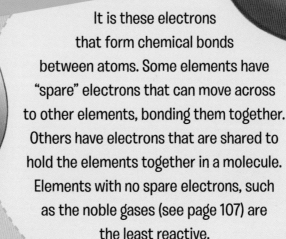

It is these electrons that form chemical bonds between atoms. Some elements have "spare" electrons that can move across to other elements, bonding them together. Others have electrons that are shared to hold the elements together in a molecule. Elements with no spare electrons, such as the noble gases (see page 107) are the least reactive.

Heavy stuff

Did you know that some water is heavier than other water? It is all about the hydrogen atoms that make up the H_2O. It looks and smells the same as regular water, but its chemical formula is D_2O (the D stands for a special kind of hydrogen, named deuterium). Read on to discover the weird world of isotopes ...

PROTONS AND NEUTRONS

To understand isotopes, you need to know that atoms have two types of particles in their nucleus (the middle bit). Roughly half are protons and half are neutrons. Protons have a positive charge, and neutrons have no charge. Atoms of a particular element all have the same number of protons, so hydrogen atoms have one, oxygen has eight, and gold has seventy-nine. That's partly what makes them all different elements.

Changes in the nucleus of an atom can make an element radioactive.

A SPECIAL CASE

Although the number of protons stays the same for a single element, the number of neutrons can vary. This gives us isotopes—different versions of the same element. Commonly, hydrogen has a single proton but no neutrons. However, a very small percentage (about 1 in 20 million) of hydrogen atoms have two neutrons. This is the isotope of hydrogen known as deuterium. When these combine with oxygen they make "heavy water."

Hydrogen has a third isotope with three neutrons, called tritium. Hydrogen is the only element with commonly used names for its isotopes.

DUAL EXISTENCE

Scientists did not know about isotopes until they began to investigate why some elements are radioactive. Frederick Soddy (1877–1956) suggested the idea in 1913, stating that certain elements can exist in two or more forms. Modern knowledge allows scientists to use isotopes to treat cancer, test substances to tell how many hundreds or thousands of years old they are, to power spacecraft, and develop smoke detectors to save lives.

Talking trash

Science is always on the move, refining its discoveries, and inventing new products and processes. Not all scientific revelations are good news. The understanding of radioactivity led to the development of the nuclear bomb, and a more recent, successful invention has led to other problems—plastics, still used today.

FANTASTIC PLASTIC?

Plastic is a man-made material, produced by joining together long chains of molecules. These molecules make up a tough, waterproof substance that can be shaped while soft and then made into solid objects. Plastic was invented in the late 1800s, and used in large amounts from around the time of World War II. Although it is an extremely practical and useful substance, making it uses large amounts of fossil fuels as raw materials. Its ingredients are natural gas and petroleum, and these cannot be replaced once we have used them up.

Large amounts of waste plastic find their way into the ocean and endanger sea life. It kills a million seabirds and 100,000 marine mammals every year.

A LONG-TERM PROBLEM

Plastic does not occur in nature, and it takes a long time to break down. Once it is made, it sticks around for hundreds of years. A plastic bag, for example, takes 500 to 1,000 years to decompose in landfill, and a plastic bottle lasts up to 450 years. And more than 1 million plastic bags are used every minute around the world. The challenge for today's scientists is how to reuse and recycle it efficiently, to prevent our planet becoming clogged up with the stuff.

There are more than 10,000 different types of plastics.

SPACE JUNK

It isn't just the planet that is full of waste. Science has allowed us to explore space, but we leave our rubbish there, too. There are around 7,500 tons of "space junk" including bits of rocket and broken satellites, and items that astronauts have dropped. British scientists are developing a special spacecraft that will collect the debris and drag it back to Earth where it should burn up on entering the atmosphere.

Space junk can cause serious damage to spacecraft and satellites.

MYTH BUSTERS

Here are two things many people believe or once believed about elements, both of which are actually just a little bit ... wrong.

Things don't burn because of phlogiston!

Until the 1780s, it was thought that things burned if they contained an invisible substance with no smell, taste, or mass. Alchemists called this substance "phlogiston" and said it was released during combustion (burning). After all the phlogiston was used up in a substance, it would not burn any more. It was only in the 1800s that it was accepted that the element oxygen is needed for things to burn, and that the air around the burning substance supplies it.

Oxygen isn't combustible!

So, if oxygen makes things burn, can large amounts of it catch fire? No! Oxygen itself does not burn. If it did, the whole room would explode whenever someone strikes a match. Instead, oxygen makes other things burn under the right circumstances. A fire needs three things—fuel (for example wood, paper, or oil), heat, and an oxidizer (which is what oxygen is) to help the chemical reaction. If you can cut off the oxygen supply (by smothering the fire) the flames will go out.

HALL OF FAME

Over the centuries, many brilliant men and women have tried to understand the world around them. And as they have worked to satisfy their own curiosity, what they have discovered has changed the world. Thanks to the work of Galileo from the sixteenth century, we know now that the Earth orbits the Sun and we have developed telescopes that let us study the stars in galaxies beyond our own. Due to the observations of Louis Pasteur from the nineteenth century, we know that germs cause disease and have developed ways to protect ourselves. Charles Darwin put forward the idea of natural selection, and Mary Anning found fossils of dinosaurs, creatures from a world unlike our own.

The scientists who have brought us such understanding often struggled and took great risks. Humphrey Davy injured himself in an experiment, and Marie Curie was eventually poisoned by her work. But they let nothing stand in their way. What mattered for them was knowledge, and they wanted to find out more.

Science comes from the Latin word "scientia," meaning knowledge. Science offers explanations that can be tested or theories that can be predicted, and scientists today make progress by building on the breakthroughs of previous years.

115

CAROLINE HERSCHEL (1750–1848)
AND WILLIAM HERSCHEL (1738–1822)

William Herschel was born in Germany in 1738, and his sister Caroline followed in 1750. Together they made enormous leaps forward in astronomy.

Trained as a musician, William moved to England to teach music. However, his great love was his hobby of building telescopes and studying the skies, with expert help from Caroline. She became the first woman to be paid for her contribution to science, and the first to discover a comet. Between them, they discovered and documented around 5,000 space objects, including eight comets, three nebulae—as well as double stars, new moons, and galaxies. William also discovered infrared radiation, and the planet Uranus—the first new planet discovered in 170 years. This act earned William the title of Royal Astronomer, for which he was paid, allowing him to quit his job and concentrate wholly on astronomy.

EDWIN HUBBLE (1889–1953)

We used to think that our galaxy, the Milky Way, was the extent of the Universe. Edwin Hubble changed all that.

Observing several dust clouds (nebulae) in outer space, he realized that they were too far away to be in the Milky Way Galaxy and that they must be in galaxies of their own. Later still, Hubble provided the evidence that proves that our universe is expanding, meaning that all the stars and planets are moving away from each other.

MARIO J. MOLINA (1943–PRESENT)

Molina's first experiments were carried out at home, in a bathroom which he converted into a laboratory. Helped by Esther Molina, his aunt and a chemist herself, he pushed himself to understand university-level studies before his eleventh birthday. Molina's breakthrough work in his adult life has helped to stop the destruction of the ozone layer. This part of the Earth's upper atmosphere plays a vital role in preventing ultraviolet radiation from reaching the ground and causing huge damage to living things. It has been destroyed in some areas by chlorofluorocarbons (CFCs) contained in spray cans and refrigerators. Molina spoke out to the science world and the media about the effects of CFCs, and he continues his work on chemistry and the environment to this day.

MARY ANNING (1799–1847)

Mary Anning was the daughter of an English couple who were too poor to send her to school. Mary learned to read and write at church, little knowing that her future discoveries would put her in front of some of the world's most important scientists.

Mary and her brother regularly searched for fossils on the beach near their home on England's south coast. When Mary was only 12, her brother discovered the head of an ichthyosaur. Mary very carefully unearthed the complete 10-m-(33-ft)-long skeleton and carried it home. She later uncovered a near-perfect plesiosaur and many other valuable fossils that were bought by leading paleontologists. The skeletons she found led to new theories about the history of the Earth and how the creatures on it may have evolved.

CARL LINNAEUS (1707–1778)

Known as the Prince of Botanists, Carl Linnaeus loved plants and flowers even as a child.

In 1735, he wrote *Systema Naturae*, in which he outlined a way to classify and identify everything in the natural world. Called "binomial nomenclature," his system creates a name composed of two parts— genus and species. A daisy, for example is the species "*perennis*" of the genus "*Bellis*"—*Bellis perennis*.

CHARLES DARWIN (1809–1882)

As a child, Darwin preferred science to classics and languages, and he was sent to university to study medicine. Unfortunately, Charles hated the sight of blood, so he swapped courses to study theology.

After graduating, Darwin set sail on a five-year journey on board the HMS *Beagle*, examining the wildlife of the world.

His studies of nature got him thinking, and after years of investigation (and conversations with biologist Alfred Russel Wallace), Darwin finally dared to publish his ideas on evolution. Darwin argued that natural selection meant successful characteristics passed from one generation to the next. His book, *On the Origin of Species* (1859) made many people angry, as many simply did not believe the theory that all species on Earth evolved from simple life forms. His ideas stood up to the challenges thrown at them, however, and gradually changed the way humans saw themselves.

GALILEO (1564–1642)

Without Galileo, there may have never been any Newtonian laws of motion (see page 54-57). Born in 1564 in Pisa, Italy, he first studied medicine at university, but switched to philosophy and mathematics.

Among his many achievements were the building of an advanced telescope, calculations on gravity and acceleration, and (like Archimedes) insisting that the laws of nature could be described mathematically. He died in 1642, the year that Isaac Newton was born.

Several of Galileo's ideas were controversial in the time in which he lived, and they got him into trouble with the Church. He insisted that the Earth moved around the Sun, not the other way around, and was sentenced to imprisonment in his own house. He continued his studies, and his work became so important that he is nicknamed the "father of modern physics."

ARCHIMEDES (287–212 BCE)

Commonly known as a mathematician, Archimedes was one of the greatest thinkers in Ancient Greece, and contributed many things to the world of science. He lived in Sicily, and is credited with figuring out how to measure the volume of an object by putting it in water (although it is untrue that he ran naked through the streets after having a bath, shouting, "Eureka!").

Not many people can claim to have invented whole new branches of science, but Archimedes can. His work on mechanics, studying liquids and gravity, was groundbreaking, and it directly influenced great minds such as Galileo and Newton. Archimedes discovered the laws of levers and pulleys. He applied mathematics to reveal laws of nature and paved the way for the science of physics. Sadly, he was killed by a Roman soldier.

BLAISE PASCAL (1623–1662)

As a young man, Pascal was a talented mathematician who invented a calculator to help his father with the tax calculations for their French hometown of Rouen. However, it was Pascal's experiments with air pressure that really made his name.

During his studies in Paris and also high in the French Alps, he invented a hydraulic press and a syringe. His principle of pressure in fluids is a vital piece of knowledge for scuba divers in the twenty-first century, preventing damage to their body at increased depths. His legacy also lives on in the casino, as he may have accidentally invented the roulette wheel while trying to make a perpetual motion machine!

MARIE CURIE (1867–1934)

At university, Marie Curie was very diligent— sometimes, she studied for so long that she fainted from hunger.

With her husband Pierre, she identified the elements radium and polonium, and noticed that radium destroyed cancerous cells. During World War I, she developed mobile X-ray units that meant soldiers could be operated on as quickly as possible. She was the first female receipient of a Nobel Prize, and her achievements helped pave the way for other women scientists.

WILHELM RÖNTGEN (1845–1923)

Born in 1845 in Prussia (now Germany), Wilhelm Röntgen spent his childhood in the Netherlands. He was expelled from school, and prevented from enrolling at other schools nearby. He had to apply to a college in Zurich, Switzerland, to continue his education.

In spite of these obstacles, Röntgen became highly thought of as a professor of physics. He studied heat and electricity, and it was while experimenting with electric currents in a glass tube that he discovered X-rays. His first images were of metal objects and the bones in his wife's hand. His findings were a breakthrough, both in wave-theory for physics and in non-invasive studies for medicine. He refused to take out a patent, so that people could benefit from his work without cost, but was nearly bankrupt when he died in 1923.

LOUIS PASTEUR (1822–1895)

The discoveries of this French chemist have saved millions of lives. He developed a theory about germs that changed medicine, and a process named after him is still used to keep food and drink safe for consumption.

Louis Pasteur was born in 1822 and as a child, he loved art and singing. As a teenager, however, he was drawn toward science. His early experiments involved beer, wine, and milk. He proved that micro-organisms, or germs, could make them go off. Heating the liquid killed the germs and preserved the drinks; this process is now known as pasteurization. Pasteur then began to study the role of germs in diseases. His first vaccines were for animals, but he continued his work to develop vaccines against diseases in humans. He also encouraged medical staff to keep their hands and equipment clean and germ-free, which was a novel idea in the 1800s.

LORD KELVIN (WILLIAM THOMSON, 1824–1907)

Born in 1824, William Thomson was so important to science that he was made a British Lord in 1892. He was not only a great thinker, but excelled at solving practical problems. He applied for patents for more than 70 inventions and wrote more than 600 scientific papers on a wide range of topics.

Kelvin's name is given to the temperature scale that he invented. He proposed it in 1848, to provide a way of describing extremely low temperatures. He created Britain's first physics laboratory in Glasgow, where he worked on the second law of thermodynamics, stating that heat will not pass from a cold body to a hotter one. He also invented many electrical instruments, had the first home in Glasgow to be lit by electric light, and advised on the laying of first telegraph cables to run under the Atlantic.

Kelvin went to Cambridge University, but shocked his father by using his university allowance to buy a boat!

J.J. THOMSON (1856–1940)

J.J. Thomson (unrelated to Lord Kelvin!) was only 14 years old when he went to university. He was the first person to suggest the existence of particles smaller than an atom and discovered the electron. Thomson was awarded the 1906 Nobel Prize in Physics for his discovery.

He also found the first evidence that stable elements can exist as isotopes and invented one of the most powerful tools in analytical chemistry—the mass spectrometer. Thirty years after J.J. Thomson was awarded his Nobel Prize, his son George won the same prize. George's prize was also for work with electrons, which he proved can behave like waves.

ALBERT EINSTEIN (1879–1955)

Many great minds have puzzled over the speed of light (see pages 88-89), but none greater than the mind of German mathematician and physicist Albert Einstein (1879-1955). He overturned the work of some of the previous centuries' greatest scientists.

Einstein is best known for his theory of relativity, expressed by the equation $E=mc^2$. In this equation, "c" is the constant speed of light in a vacuum. Einstein was such a great thinker that he examined the possibility of strange things happening as you get closer to this speed, such as the slowing down of time. His life was not an easy one. His schoolteachers said he was badly behaved and not that bright. He tried and failed to get a job as a teacher, and ended up working in an office. However, once he began to publish scientific papers, the world began to take notice. In 1999 he was named the Person of the Century by *Time* magazine.

Einstein received the Nobel Prize for his work on light, but not for his more famous theories of relativity.

JOSEPH PRIESTLEY (1733–1804) AND CARL WILHELM SCHEELE (1742–1786)

Scientific history is not always straightforward and clear-cut. Often, several great minds reach the same conclusions, with different methods and in different places.

Take these two chemists, for example. Joseph Priestley (1733–1804) is often credited with the discovery of oxygen in 1774. However, Carl Wilhelm Scheele (1742–1786) isolated the gas before then, in 1772. Unfortunately for Scheele, Priestley published his findings first. Neither of these scientists actually called the element oxygen. Another great chemist, Antoine Lavoisier, named it in 1779.

Scheele was a great thinker. He discovered another five elements that he received no credit for, because although he predicted their existence, he did not succeed in preparing them in his laboratory. Perhaps more famously, Scheele was known for testing poisonous chemicals on himself!

Joseph Priestley also invented fizzy drinks! He created soda water in 1767 by adding CO_2 to water.

HUMPHRY DAVY (1778–1829)

Humphry Davy was knighted in 1812 for his research and inventions. He was fascinated by gases, and was known to inhale laughing gas (nitrous oxide) to study its effects. He nearly killed himself by accidentally inhaling a type of fuel known as water gas.

Davy changed the lives of miners in the 1800s with his invention of the safety lamp, which prevented fatal explosions underground. His work on electric currents led to the isolation of sodium, potassium, and calcium. He is also linked to the discovery or naming of magnesium, strontium, barium, boron, chlorine, and iodine—an extraordinary number of elements, considering that only 42 were known before then.

A lecture given by Davy about Galvanism was the inspiration for Mary Shelley's classic book, *Frankenstein* (1818).

MARIA THE JEWESS (UNKNOWN)

Maria lived between the first and third centuries, and her name (in French) lives on in her invention, the *bain-marie*.

Still used today, in both the laboratory and the kitchen, the bain-marie ensures that only a gentle, indirect heat is applied. Her writings no longer exist, but they had a great influence on early alchemists.

GLOSSARY

atmosphere
The layers of gases around a planet.

cell
The smallest unit a living thing is made from.

embryo
A partially developed living thing, for example an unborn baby.

evolve
To gradually change and develop over time.

extinct
Having no living members left.

force
Energy that makes an object move.

galaxy
A system of millions of stars, gas and dust held together by gravity.

genes
A combination of molecules that give a living thing its characteristics.

gravity
A force that pulls an object toward a larger object.

flammable
Describing a substance that burns easily.

mass
The amount of matter (stuff) that something is made of.

neuron
A specialist nerve cell that passes impulses.

orbit
The curved path of a body around another body (like the Moon around the Earth).

organ
A part of the body that has a specific, vital job to do.

organism
An individual living thing.

prehistoric
Before written historical records.

temperature
The amount of heat energy present.

tissue
A specific type of material that makes a living thing.

vacuum
A space with no particles (solid, liquid, or gas) in it.

weight
The force exerted on a body by gravity.